A VIABLE SUSPECT

THE STORY OF MULTIPLE MURDERS AND HOW A POLICE FORCE'S REACH PROVED TOO SHORT FOR CANADA'S MOST NOTORIOUS COLD CASE

BARRY RUHL

Sgt. (Ret.) Ontario Provincial Police

FriesenPress

Suite 300 – 990 Fort Street
Victoria, BC, Canada V8V 3K2
www.friesenpress.com

ISBN
978-1-4602-4744-0 (Hardcover)
978-1-4602-4745-7 (Paperback)
978-1-4602-4746-4 (eBook)

1. True Crime, Murder, Serial Killers

Distributed to the trade by The Ingram Book Company

Table of Contents

DEDICATION v

INTRODUCTION ix

CHAPTER 1 — TO SERVE, PROTECT, AND SURVIVE 1

CHAPTER 2 — ARRESTED DEVELOPMENT 21

CHAPTER 3 — PRIME SUSPECT 37

CHAPTER 4 — THE EPIPHANY 45

CHAPTER 5 — ON THE ROAD AGAIN 69

CHAPTER 6 — RETIRED AND REHIRED 77

CHAPTER 7 — A PERSON OF DISINTEREST 97

CHAPTER 8 — THE KAUFMAN INQUIRY 111

CHAPTER 9 — LAST CHANCE FOR JUSTICE 121

CHAPTER 10 — LAST CALL 133

CHAPTER 11 — A VIABLE SUSPECT BEYOND REACH 145

FOOTNOTES 161

REFERENCES 171

TIME LINE — THE 1997 REPORT 175

ACKNOWLEDGEMENTS. 179

PHOTO CREDITS 181

AUTHOR'S PERSONAL ARCHIVE. 181

OTHER SOURCES 181

OTHER DOCUMENTS 182

DEDICATION

This book is dedicated to the Truscott family,
shackled by the scales of injustice until the truth set them free.

"I want to see justice done. Justice hasn't been done,"..."Not to the
Harper family and not to my family. So I mean for both families.
It's all I want. After forty years I don't think that's too much to ask."
Steven Truscott

A very special thanks to Laurel for her insight
encouragement and support.

"To Barry, for honouring your oath. October 2008."
Author anonymous.

INTRODUCTION

It is possible that on August 28, 2007, the day the Ontario Court of Appeal finally and formally acquitted Steven Truscott of the 1959 murder of 12-year-old Lynne Harper of Clinton, Ont., a man called Larry Talbot had more than a few qualms.

Truscott was only 14 when he was convicted and sentenced to death for Harper's murder. His sentence was subsequently commuted to life imprisonment and he was paroled after serving 10 years. After his release, his notoriety forced him to live under an assumed name in an Ontario city until March of 2000, when the CBC featured a documentary about the trial of Steven Truscott.

His acquittal may have made Talbot, a man well known to police over the years, wonder if the case — albeit almost 50 years old — might be reopened, and if a new investigation might lead police to his door.

The case had been controversial from the beginning, partly because of the ages of the victim and Truscott, partly because of the paucity of evidence against the boy, and partly because of the speed with which the investigation was conducted and the conviction handed down. Throughout the years, many people have come to Truscott's defense, and he and his legal team continued to try to prove that a miscarriage of justice had occurred.

Over the years, Talbot had been convicted of a number of lesser crimes, and was also a prime suspect in the murder of another young girl bearing a similar MO (modus operandi) to the Harper case, as well as being investigated in connection with a number of other murders of young women.

But, just over a year after Truscott's acquittal, Talbot died in an Ontario nursing home, without ever having to answer to any murder charges.

In 1997, as a retired sergeant from the Ontario Provincial Police (OPP), I wrote a detailed report in which I suggested that Talbot might be a viable suspect in several unsolved murders of which I was aware. It was not my first involvement with Talbot. In fact, in 1971, Talbot victimized my then girlfriend and me.

But my purpose in writing this book is not to garner revenge on a dead man. It is to show how a viable suspect in the Harper homicide, and other murders, may have slipped through the OPP's investigative and hierarchical cracks. I have used a pseudonym for the "person of interest," out of respect for his family's privacy and the fact that he was not charged with or convicted of any of the homicides included in the book.

CHAPTER 1

TO SERVE, PROTECT, AND SURVIVE.

My knowledge of the Ontario Provincial Police began when I was five, and visited my Uncle Jack in Brantford, Ont. Jack Whitty was my mom's brother, and commander of the Brantford OPP. He and wife Rhea lived in an apartment above the detachment and during the visit, I sneaked downstairs and watched the uniformed officers leaving the detachment in their gleaming black and white cruisers. It was a real thrill for a five-year-old. I followed Jack's career, and was especially proud when he was promoted to assistant commissioner in 1962. I think it was at that time that I considered a career in law enforcement.

In 1963, I was accepted, and in July 1964 I attended the OPP College in Toronto. At the conclusion of the three-week course, I was transferred to Port Arthur (Thunder Bay). Since I'd never been north of Parry Sound, it seemed a long way from my home in St. Thomas, just a short drive north of Lake Erie in southern Ontario.

Longlac was one of a number of postings I had during my 30 year career. I also served at Meaford, Montreal (Expo 67),

Kitchener, Sauble Beach, Barrie, Wasaga Beach and Orillia General Headquarters.

Police officers experience a mixed bag of occurrences, ranging from the trivial calls for service to the most serious. And they remember the ones that stood out, long after they retire. There's one I vividly recall from the summer of 1971 at Sauble Beach, and ironically it occurred when I was off duty. In the middle of the night, a masked intruder, Larry Talbot*, broke into a cottage where I was staying with my fiancée. This violent encounter set the stage for a different kind of intrusion by him. He invaded my psyche, and I think about him almost daily: If he killed seventeen year old Pauline Dudley, was she the only victim or was he responsible for the death of other young women? Did he kill Lynne Harper?

My story begins at Sauble Beach, a popular summer playground, located on the shores of Lake Huron, in south western Ontario. It's a wonderful place for folks who simply want to chill, frolic on the beach and enjoy time with family and friends.

But this wasn't Larry Talbot's idea of fun. Instead, this was his opportunity to prey on those unsuspecting tourists. Welcome to Sauble Beach!

This sign welcomes thousands of visitors to the
Lake Huron resort town of Sauble Beach

In June 1969, I was transferred to Sauble Beach, for the summer and it was a welcome relief from patrolling the busy highways in the

Kitchener-Waterloo areas. I was assigned to foot patrol in the downtown area and the beach. It was an easy assignment and I enjoyed mingling with the vacationers liberated from their usual routines.

There were a variety of concessions on the main street and the merchandise included racks of risqué swim suits, sloganed T-shirts, and cheap jewelry. There was also a tattoo parlour and, on the beach, a myriad of fast food concessions. Offerings included pizza, hotdogs, hamburgers, French fries smothered in gravy, and that irresistible pink candy floss. The beach was like a magnet, pulling the vacationers to its pristine waters, young families struggling with wagons, women in colourful swimsuits with partners lugging coolers, and seniors with fond memories of yesteryears on the sands.

To a large extent, the folks visiting Sauble Beach were law abiding. The only time we were concerned that summer was when an outlaw motorcycle gang rode into town on their "crotch rockets." I knew the gang's leader, who grew up in St. Thomas, a couple of blocks from where I lived. We stopped them at the main intersection and I approached the leader. "Hey Johnny, what's happening?" He immediately recognized me and we chatted a bit.

After some small talk, his female companion looked at him, and then somewhat disappointedly at me, and said, "So what happened to you?" The bikers behaved themselves during their stay at the beach.

As much as I enjoyed the beat, I was one happy cop when the detachment commander assigned me to investigate thefts occurring at the north end of the beach. In one case, the complainant reported $100 missing, and she was certain the money was in her wallet when she went to bed. I walked the perimeter of the cottage and didn't see any signs of an entry, but discovered faint footprints beneath the bedroom window she left open at night. How could the culprit have stolen the money without having entered her bedroom?

During the investigation, I met a local businessman who had resided for most of his life at Sauble Beach. I asked if he knew anyone who could be responsible for the thefts. "Well there's one guy you might want to check," he answered. "His name's Larry Talbot, and he's had a cottage at the beach for years. Some of his neighbours told me he takes walks late at night." He also recalled that when Talbot was a teenager, he was caught peeking in a window and watching a woman undress. He was wearing a mask and was picked up by the OPP, but the man didn't think he was charged because of his youth. He showed me where Talbot lived, and it was close to the theft I investigated.

As a result of this conversation, Talbot was included as a "person of interest" in the investigation because of his familiarity with the surrounding neighborhoods, his late-night walks, and his voyeuristic past. Talbot was 41 and married with two children. He had been raised in Scarborough, completed Grade 10, and left school to work as a salesman in Toronto. It only lasted for a year and he worked at other jobs before obtaining employment with Industrial Plumbing, a Toronto-based company. Talbot drove a 1971 Ford registered to his company. He lived in Scarborough and stayed at the cottage during the summer months. He had one criminal conviction in Hamilton for theft under $50.

During my midnight shifts, I would pass his cottage and one night I spotted him standing by a kitchen table reading a paper. I had a better look at Talbot a couple of weeks later, when I was walking along the beach. He was about 5'9" or 5'10", medium build, with short dark brown hair. He was wearing a bathing suit and appeared to be in good shape. He was sitting by the water, but didn't have the usual amenities one takes to the beach, and appeared to be staring at a young couple 15 metres or so away.

I had enough information about Talbot and needed to decide when to watch him. I checked the occurrence books and found three more cottage thefts similar to the one I was investigating. I got approval from my boss, and the following Tuesday evening, Const. Paul Farroll and I hunkered down on the ground near his cottage. The only signs of life were the crickets chirping and the occasional rustling of critters in the bushes. The lights were on but there wasn't any sign of Talbot. Suddenly, Paul started thrashing. "I think a snake just crawled over my legs!" he exclaimed. I couldn't help but laugh, but with that, our first night of surveillance went south.

We used a cruiser the following night. I suspect Paul was happier with this decision. I was familiar with the area and found a location 150 metres north of Talbot's cottage. If he went for a walk, we'd spot him.

It was quiet and we were about to call it a night about 3:30 a.m., when suddenly we spotted a figure coming out of the bushes approximately 60 metres south of us. He was walking fast, headed in our direction. "Wait until he's close and hit him with the lights," I told Paul. When the shadowy figure was 30 metres or so away, Paul turned on the lights and a startled Larry Talbot stopped and stared at us like a deer caught in the headlights. He was carrying a long pole. Suddenly he turned and ran into the bushes on the west side of the road. We chased him but he managed to escape in the thick underbrush. We searched the area and found a mop handle. I realized this would be an ideal and clever tool to use to hook a purse through an open window, steal the money and return it to the residence.

Paul and I discussed our next move. If we approached him, he'd probably have a ready explanation for the pole, such as using it to protect himself from dogs or as a walking stick. We were also skating on thin ice because Talbot wasn't near a cottage when we spotted him. We decided to back off and periodically watch him.

The remaining summer was relatively quiet. There were no other thefts reported and if Talbot was the culprit, his close encounter with us may have prompted him to curtail his activities. I wondered if he experienced any sleepless nights worried we were going to pay him a visit.

The following year I returned to the beach and hoped Talbot wouldn't be up to his old tricks. I periodically checked the occurrence books for cottage thefts and in the first few weeks, none were reported in the vicinity of the previous thefts. This was about to change.

On July 16 at 3 a.m., I was dispatched to a home invasion at the north end of the beach. I met a distraught woman staying at a cottage with her two children. She said she'd been asleep when a man wearing a mask entered her bedroom and stood over her.

He shone a flashlight in her face and was wearing a disguise she described as a "white Halloween mask." The intruder told her to keep quiet, took her purse to the living room and rummaged through it. A short time later he fled and she called the police.

The victim was unable to describe the perpetrator. I searched the grounds around the cottage and discovered a size nine footprint next to the front steps and the door propped open with a piece of wood. The location of the cottage invasion was almost behind Talbot's cottage on an adjacent street.

I decided I couldn't question Talbot because there was nothing specific tying him to the incident. If Talbot was the culprit, I was hoping he'd eventually make a mistake. That day came the very next summer, when he broke into the cottage where I was sleeping.

I normally stayed at the Kit Wat Motel with other officers, but this particular June week, I rented a cottage across from the motel because my fiancée, Pat, was on holidays from her job in public relations at CIL in Toronto and was visiting me for the week. The sexual revolution of the1960s had not yet worked its way into the code of behaviour acceptable for police officers, and most nights during Pat's visit we slept separately. But one night I decided to sleep at the cottage with her.

The rear door point of entry.

A loud noise woke me out of a deep sleep. My first groggy and irritable thought was that some of the other cops were playing a prank on us. But as I stumbled out of bed, stark naked, toward the bedroom wall light switch, I almost bumped into a dark figure in the doorway — a man in a garish orange mask holding a flashlight and pointing a gun at my face. This was no joke, and this wasn't one of my cop pals.

"What's up buddy?" I asked cautiously. There was silence as the armed intruder stared at us and slowly backed into the living room.

Then he uttered a terrifying command: "Get the bride out here!"

"Leave her out of this!" I replied. Suddenly, Pat appeared wearing a short, slinky nightgown. In a gruff voice, the intruder ordered her to raise it.

Pat, in a timid, almost inaudible voice replied, "I don't think so."

He pointed the menacing gun. "Lift it or I'll shoot!"

The engagement photograph of Pat.

Trembling, she slowly raised it. The intruder lifted and lowered the gun in an unspoken command to make her move faster and as she raised the gown, he was thrusting his hips as if he was having sex. "Come on, come on that's it, that's it!"

Suddenly he stopped and ordered Pat to get my wallet. She retrieved it from the mantle and was walking towards him when I grabbed it and threw it on the floor. By now he was standing at the rear door and ordered me to pick it up. "No!" I said.

He pointed the gun at me. "Pick it up or I'll shoot!"

"I don't think you will!" I replied. He stared at me for a second and then bolted from the cottage, grabbing Pat's purse as he fled. I went after him, chasing him south along King Edward Drive.

It must have been a surreal spectacle for any fortunate (unfortunate?) enough to have witnessed it, a masked man being pursued by a naked man.

"Get back!" he yelled. Suddenly, he turned and fired a shot, hitting me in the chest but not stopping me. I managed to grab the back of his coat and he swung around and struck me several times with the gun. I was injured but managed to wrestle him to the ground. I got on top of him and he attempted to get up but I pummeled him until he surrendered. "Let me go. Don't call the cops!" he pleaded.

I removed the mask and immediately recognized him. "I am a cop, Talbot, and you're under arrest!"

Pat, meanwhile, had run to the motel and woke Cpl. Ron Love. Ron grabbed his gun and handcuffs, and when he arrived, helped me cuff Talbot. An examination of Talbot's gun showed it to be a powerful pellet gun. Pat's purse was recovered from a nearby ditch.

I've been in a number of fights, but none like the one I had with Talbot. He pistol-whipped me in a manner that convinced me this wasn't his first time using the weapon. It was very fortunate I had stayed overnight with Pat.

When we arrived at the detachment — I was dressed by this time — I took a good look at Talbot, who had a black eye. My injuries were relatively minor, including a gash to my nose and a flesh wound from the pellet shot. I asked him if he wanted to make a statement and he angrily replied, "Why do you want a statement? You got the gun!"

The following morning, the Identification Unit arrived from the OPP detachment in Mount Forest, about 100 kilometres away. They took photographs of the crime scene, including the rear door of the cottage with a broken window pane, and concluded he had broken the window (the loud noise I heard) so he could reach in and unlock the door. They also photographed a pail he had used to prop the door open, presumably so he could make a hasty exit, and the clothes he was wearing — dark blue jacket, work pants, running shoes and leather gloves. He wasn't wearing underwear or socks. His mask had been made by cutting three holes in an orange industrial cloth, and he had used butcher cord to fasten it to his head.

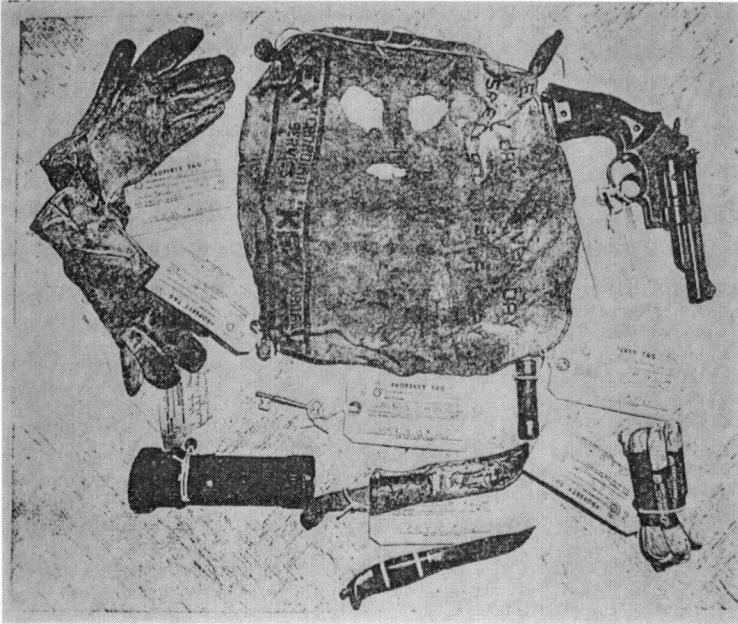

Burglary items seized from Talbot.

He was also carrying four sets of hockey skate laces, a skeleton key, and a sharp hunting knife, elements of what police call a rape kit.

Talbot's car was located 0.3 kilometres from our cottage, parked in front of a vacant cottage that was for sale. The vehicle's keys were stashed on top of the right front tire. Talbot's street clothes, underwear, shoes, and wallet were in the rear compartment, along with some sandwiches. The trunk contained a wooden dildo.

All of this indicated Talbot was well-organized, and had carefully planned the break-in.

Talbot was charged with armed robbery, break and enter with intent, and assault occasioning bodily harm. He was remanded to the Walkerton County Jail and en route I told him it was fortunate Pat wasn't harmed. In retrospect, I was a victim, and someone else should have questioned Talbot and escorted him to jail. He replied something to the effect of, "Well, if you'd kept the drapes closed, nothing would have happened."

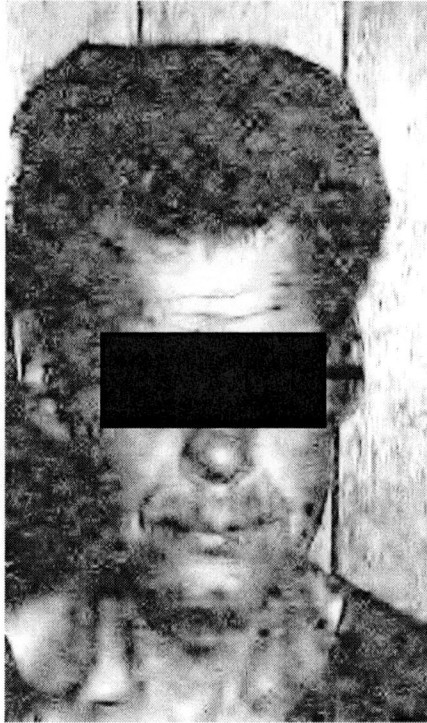

Identification Photo of Larry Talbot.

Talbot appeared before a justice of the peace and the trial was scheduled for September 21, 1971, at Walkerton. He elected to be tried by a judge without a jury.

Pat remained at the cottage for the rest of the week and when I was working several of my buddies kept her company. This was a real tough time for both of us. She was frightened and humiliated by the experience, and I felt terrible about witnessing the assault on her and being unable to intervene. That's what cops are expected to do. I couldn't lose the feeling of rage that had burned inside me as I chased him.

Pat was emotionally distraught. When she returned home, her doctor prescribed a sedative called Librium, but she didn't refill the prescription.

On the day after the break-in, Pat's parents were travelling to their cottage when they heard Gordon Sinclair announce on CFRB radio that Barry Ruhl, an OPP officer at Sauble Beach, had been shot during a cottage invasion. Pat's mom was frantic and called the detachment. An officer told her Pat had been with me during the break-in but nothing else. When Pat returned home she told her parents what happened but didn't include the fact I spent the night with her. Her father wanted to know why I was at the cottage in the middle of the night. She told him we'd had a barbecue and I went to sleep on a couch. I suppose he wanted believe her, and that was the last time he mentioned it.

I spent many anxious moments worrying that Pat would be required to testify at the trial. She was also concerned because everyone, including her parents, would discover what really happened that night. But If Talbot entered a not guilty plea, her testimony would be required.

My fears were eliminated when Talbot appeared at Provincial Court in Walkerton on September 21, 1971 before Judge H.C. Mosser. Talbot was represented by W.T Stayshyn and Howard Hines from Hamilton, and entered a plea of "guilty" to the charge of armed robbery. In an attempt to mitigate the sentence, Talbot's legal team presented a psychiatric report prepared by Dr. A.J. Renton who assessed Talbot and didn't believe he would be recidivistic. There were also a number of "character witnesses" who testified the Larry Talbot they knew was a good person and gave examples of the positive things they remembered about him.

The following is a relevant part of Judge Mosser's summation:

> Mr. Talbot, I have had the opportunity to peruse
> the reports of Dr. Renton and to consider carefully
> the statements made by counsel and the character
> evidence of your friends, which is all very favor-
> able. These people have travelled a long way to say
> many good things and yet when you consider what
> happened at Sauble Beach, it must be shattering
> for the people who live in the area to learn that
> something like this can happen to someone who is
> a very kindly person and a very model citizen. This
> makes sentencing very difficult. From Dr. Renton's
> report there is little likelihood of you repeating the

act that took place at Sauble Beach and there is
very little likelihood that anyone in the immediate
vicinity of Sauble Beach is going to be imperiled if
you are given a suspended sentence and a probation-
ary period.[1]

Mosser found Talbot guilty as charged and he was given a suspended sentence with two years' probation. He was also prohibited
from returning to Sauble Beach for two years and prohibited from
possessing firearms of any kind for the same period of time. The
charges of break and enter with intent and assault occasioning
bodily harm were withdrawn.

Pat and I were extremely shocked and disappointed. This didn't
seem like justice to us, and as it turned out, the judge and psychiatrist couldn't have been more wrong.

There was another unpleasant surprise awaiting when my supervisor subsequently ordered me to submit a report explaining what I
was doing in a cottage with a woman who wasn't my wife at 4:30
in the morning. In a sense, I felt *I* was on trial. I was very upset at
this intrusion but reluctantly submitted the report. When I didn't
hear anything, I assumed the investigation was concluded and my
Victorian faux pas was forgiven. I suspect since Pat and I were
engaged to be married the following year that "case" was closed. I've
often wondered what the punishment would have been if they'd
found me "guilty."

Ironically, I received a "letter of commendation" from OPP
Comm. Eric Silk on December 13, 1971[2] congratulating me for the
"courage" I displayed in arresting an "armed intruder." The letter is
hanging on the wall in my study, beside a picture of me with Steven
Truscott taken at his residence in Guelph on July 1, 2007, when the
Truscotts hosted a garden party for their supporters.

Steven Truscott and Barry Ruhl at Steven's residence in Guelph on July 1, 2007.

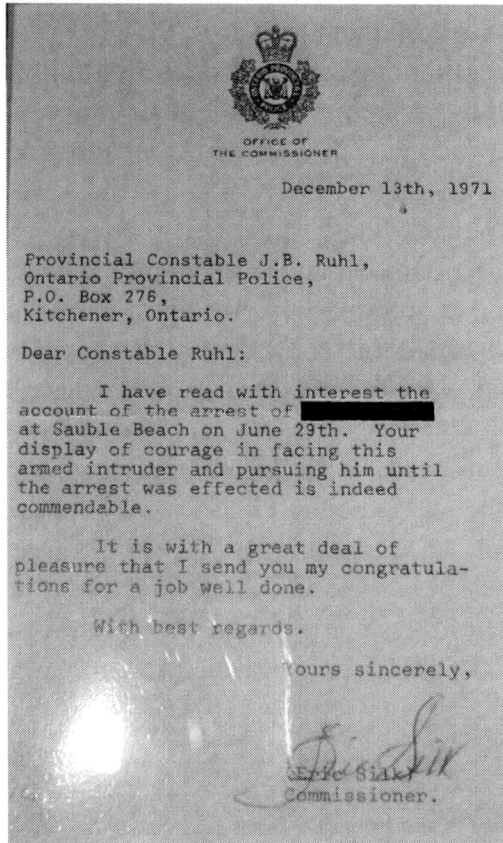

OFFICE OF
THE COMMISSIONER

December 13th, 1971

Provincial Constable J.B. Ruhl,
Ontario Provincial Police,
P.O. Box 276,
Kitchener, Ontario.

Dear Constable Ruhl:

I have read with interest the account of the arrest of ▮▮▮▮▮▮▮ at Sauble Beach on June 29th. Your display of courage in facing this armed intruder and pursuing him until the arrest was effected is indeed commendable.

It is with a great deal of pleasure that I send you my congratulations for a job well done.

With best regards.

Yours sincerely,

Eric Silk
Commissioner.

Letter of commendation from Comm. E.H. Silk following Larry Talbot's arrest.

Following the break-in at our cottage, I returned to work and to a large extent the remaining summer months were quiet. When I returned to Kitchener in the fall, I sent an intelligence report to Mount Forest District Headquarters regarding Talbot. I wanted it disseminated to personnel assigned to the beach, and it included my belief that Talbot would continue to prey on cottagers. My hunch was right, although it wasn't confirmed for several years.

On October 11, 1978, just after 10 p.m., a woman at a Sauble Beach cottage on Second Avenue North saw a man staring at her through the bedroom window. She yelled and he fled. About an hour later, a man was arrested near his car, which was parked outside a vacant cottage on the same street. It was Larry Talbot, and the following items were seized from him:

- A loaded pellet gun
- A hunting knife
- Two silk stockings (mask)
- A roll of tape
- A pair of gloves
- A two-cell black flashlight
- Pliers
- Bolt cutters
- Two adjustable wrenches
- A pair of Adidas running shoes (painted black)

He was also wearing size nine shoes, the same size as the perpetrator in the 1970 cottage invasion, when the woman staying at a cottage with her two children was terrorized.

On May 15, 1979, Talbot pleaded guilty to possession of burglary tools and was sentenced to six months in jail in Toronto. I had previously been contacted by the Crown Attorney, who said details of our cottage invasion would be included at the trial if Talbot pleaded not guilty. This would be introduced to show premeditation and is called "similar fact evidence." As it turned out, it wasn't required.

Less than three months later, there was a truly curious incident at Sauble. On August 5, at 9:15 a.m., a cottager returned to his residence and discovered a male asleep in his bedroom. He woke the intruder up and asked what he was doing there and why he was carrying a knife in a sheath and wearing leather golf gloves. The intruder said his name was Dawson and he was returning from a party and must have entered the wrong house.

After drinking a glass of water and taking some Aspirin, he left. But when the owner checked, he discovered his solitaire ring missing, as well as coin sets, a gentleman's gold watch, a Craftsman bench grinder, protective eye glasses and some American currency. He also noticed a turkey and a roast had been moved from the basement freezer to the refrigerator. And he found two quarts of frozen milk in plastic containers, with the corners cut off, in the sink. It looked like his visitor had planned an extended stay.

When the investigating officer checked the crime scene, he discovered entry was gained by forcing the locked vent windows. He also noted that everything disturbed by the intruder had either been put back in place or cleaned up. The culprit had also placed a large towel on the bed and set the alarm clock for10:30 a.m.

On September 1, 1979, just after midnight, Talbot was stopped by police in Sauble Beach. He was on a weekend pass from the Community Resources Centre, Stanford House in Toronto, where he was completing a six-month sentence. But the restrictions on his weekend pass included that he was not to leave the Toronto area, was not to drive, and had to surrender his Temporary Absence Permit if stopped by the police.

When the trunk of his vehicle was searched, police found a pair of golf gloves, along with "other house-breaking tools" not specified in the police report. Police then learned Talbot was also on a Temporary Absence Permit at the time of the August 5 break-in and "sleep-in." A partial fingerprint lifted from the site of the August incident was matched to Talbot.

On September 8, Talbot admitted breaking into the cottage and stealing the property. The watch was found in his desk drawer. He said he sold the coins and threw the grinder in the garbage. The ring was found at his residence. On September 25, he pleaded guilty to the break-in and received a one-year sentence consecutive to the six months he was given for possession of burglary tools.

When I reviewed the investigating officer's report many years later, two things stood out: Talbot was carrying a knife and wearing gloves, and he cleaned up the mess when he broke into the cottage. During my career, I never investigated a break-in where the perpetrator cleaned up.

I've always believed Talbot committed a number of crimes and wasn't caught. One such incident occurred June 1, 1978, when a break-in happened at a cottage previously owned by Talbot, but occupied that night by a young female teacher. The only sign of entry was severed telephone lines. But the intruder had rummaged through her purse and stole $20.

The following day, the teacher received a call at school from a man who told her he had watched her sleeping, that she had "nice knockers" and he was going to "rape" her, but wanted her to be a "willing participant."

I requested a discreet check at Talbot's company office in Toronto and was advised he was probably in the Sauble Beach area at the time of the entry but the investigating officer never questioned him about the break-in. However, following the 1979 break-in at the cottage (where the owner found Talbot sleeping in his bed), Talbot's sister and brother-in-law told his probation official they strongly believed he may have stolen from the cottage he previously owned.[3]

A second case went all the way back to 1969, two years before he woke me in the middle of the night, and involved the violent assault and rape of a young woman. On August 25 of that year, the victim was hitch-hiking west of Barrie when she was picked up, taken to a secluded area east of Owen Sound, pistol whipped, forced to disrobe and raped. She was threatened with death, and the assailant took her purse and clothes before fleeing the scene. The following is a description of the suspect and the description of Talbot when he broke into our cottage.[4]

GHQ 9-69

ONTARIO PROVINCIAL POLICE

WANTED PERSON

UNKNOWN MAN WANTED FOR RAPE AND ARMED ROBBERY NEAR OWEN
SOUND, ONTARIO, AUGUST 25, 1969.

AGE: 40 to 50 years

HEIGHT: 5 feet, 8 inches

WEIGHT: Approximately 160 pounds

BUILD: Medium

HAIR: Sandy brown with reddish tinge - combed back

DRESS: Was wearing gold-coloured short sleeved shirt (had bloodstains on front), green trousers, brown leather belt with small gold buckle, green canvas shoes with white soles - red line around soles.

REMARKS: Subject was soft spoken; was calm and methodical; possibly left handed; had no apparent accent.

Composite Reproduction Of Suspect

The wanted person was driving a vehicle described as a 1969 Chevelle Malibu Two-Door Hard Top Sports Coupe, licence unknown, light green exterior and interior, conventional bench-type front seat which may be bloodstained. The auto was equipped with an automatic transmission (shift lever on steering column), custom radio, and shoulder safety harness (to slip above doors).

Following the attack, the victim's purse was taken and is still missing. The purse is described as resembling a lunch pail and is navy blue plastic, with a handle on top and a side clasp. The purse contained $20 in assorted bills, a pink compact, and personal papers including a social insurance card and a beginner's driver's licence.

Caution should be used as the suspect was armed with a black-coloured revolver with a six-inch barrel. The victim was pistol-whipped with this weapon and the assailant also threatened her with death.

Any person in possession of information regarding the identity of the wanted person herein, or circumstances surrounding the commission of this offence, should communicate immediately with the nearest police authority, or the Director, Central Records and Communications Branch, Ontario Provincial Police, Toronto, Ontario.

125 Lake Shore Blvd. East
Toronto 220, Ontario
September 9, 1969
Telephone: (416) 365-6441

ERIC SILK, Q.C.
COMMISSIONER

Subject wanted for rape, in the Owen Sound area, August 25, 1969.

SUSPECT	TALBOT
40-50 years	39 years
5' 8"	5'10"
Approx. 160 lbs.	155lbs.
Sandy brown hair-combed back	Brown hair, straight back
No accent	No accent
Struck with gun in left hand	Held gun in left hand
Struck head with gun	Struck head with gun
Purse taken	Purse taken
1969 Chevelle, light green	1969 Ford, green

Talbot was investigated in connection with the attack. Police learned he had customers in the Collingwood, Meaford and Owen Sound areas, plus the cottage at Sauble Beach.

In 1971, Talbot even appeared in an identification lineup following our break-in. However, the rape victim didn't choose him and selected a lineup volunteer instead. Witness identification has always been problematic, and in this case, the violent assault, along with the passage of time, may have prevented her from selecting Talbot, if in fact he was the attacker. Despite an intensive investigation, the case was never solved.

There are a number of unsolved homicides in Ontario, and I believe Larry Talbot should be considered a person of interest in several of them. In one particular instance, an innocent teenager was convicted of the 1959 murder of Lynne Harper. Was this Talbot's work too?

CHAPTER 2

ARRESTED DEVELOPMENT

I was enjoying a holiday with my family in Bayfield in the summer of 1959, five years before I was accepted into the OPP, when I overheard some kids talking about the murder of a young girl who lived at the Clinton Air Force Base, about 20 kilometres away. The accused killer was a 14-year old boy, Steven Truscott, also from the base. It was a sensational story, but I was only 16 myself, with other teenage priorities, and gradually, Lynne Harper's death faded from my memory while Truscott languished in the county jail at Goderich awaiting trial.

Photograph of 12 year old Lynne Harper.

I didn't become fully aware of the details of the Truscott case until I saw: His Word Against History, The Steven Truscott Story on CBC, *the fifth estate*, March 20, 2000 and read *Until You Are Dead* by Julian Sher, published in 2001. It is the compelling story of the tribulations Steven endured before, during, and after his trial, and his attempts to clear his name.

"Lynne and Steven set off for what was to become the most famous bike ride in Canadian legal history,"[1] Sher wrote.

On Tuesday, June 9, 1959, Steven ran into Lynne in a park near the public school. She asked for a ride to Highway 8 because she wanted to see the ponies at a house along the highway. They set off along the county road, passing a number of friends as they crossed the bridge above the Bayfield River, about 400 metres south of the highway. When Steven left her at the highway, he returned to the bridge and watched Lynne get into a car, headed east on Highway 8.

The county road leading to Highway Eight.

Lynne didn't return home, and the next morning her frantic father Leslie, a flying officer at the base, drove around the base asking about his daughter. One person he approached was Dan Truscott, who wasn't sure if his kids had seen Lynne and suggested he check with them. He went to the residence and learned that Steven dropped Lynne off at the highway. Harper contacted the OPP and Const. Donald Hobbs questioned Steven on Wednesday morning at school. The boy told Hobbs he took Lynne to the highway and watched her get into a late-model Chevrolet with "lots of chrome" and something yellow or orange on the rear bumper.[2]

On Thursday, June 11, Lynne's body was discovered in Lawson's Bush, which the young couple had passed as they biked toward the highway. She had been raped and strangled with her blouse. The OPP assigned 33-year-old Insp. Harold Graham to the investigation. He was considered a very capable investigator. On June 11, he arrived in Clinton, and that evening circulated a bulletin to police in Ontario. According to Julian Sher, it was the only copy in police files and was in Graham's handwriting:

Re: Lynne Harper-raped and strangled body found in [the] bush [at the] RCAF Station Clinton-believed to have taken place about 9:00 p.m., Tuesday, June 10. One witness (Truscott) reports Lynne was given a ride in a solid grey or white Chev. with yellow plates on Highway 8 going east towards Seaforth. Only the driver in the car. ... At your discretion please check white cars with yellow plates and observe occupants especially for scratches on face, neck, hands and arms.[3]

It's evident from the communiqué that Graham initially believed Lynne was murdered "about 9 p.m., June 10" (actually June 9) and the culprit could have scratches on his body. How did the police establish 9 p.m. as time of death? And why did they think the perpetrator could have scratches on his body?

The autopsy was conducted on Thursday at 7:30 p.m. by Dr. John Penistan, a pathologist from Stratford, assisted by Dr. David Brooks. It was completed in two hours and cause of death was "strangulation by ligature."

Penistan established time of death by holding a jar containing stomach contents up to a light. He testified at Steven's trial: "This stomach content, I placed in a glass jar, which was sealed in my presence, with one of my seals and given to Corporal [Hank] Sayeau." The 9 p.m. time of death in Graham's bulletin was changed, by Penistan, to "probably between seven [o'clock] and a quarter to eight."[4] This was incriminating because Steven and Lynne were together during that time.

Even as far back as 1959, holding a jar of stomach contents up to a light was an unorthodox way to establish time of death. When I attended a post mortem as an investigating police officer, I would brief the pathologist on the facts gathered during an investigation. If that was the case in this examination, it's probable the officers at Harper's post mortem, Cpl. John Erskine and Const. Jim Moore, would have told the attending physicians, among other things, the time Steven and Lynne were together. Could this information have motivated Penistan to revise the initial estimate of the time of death? We'll never know, but the change put Steven Truscott squarely in the investigators' crosshairs.

In *Until You Are Dead*, Sher wrote: "Selecting 9:00 p.m. as a possible time of death was going to create a big problem for the inspector. His chief suspect — the boy he was soon to arrest — was safe at home babysitting at the time when, according to Graham's bulletin, Lynne's assailant was murdering her. Once Graham jailed Steven, no further references to that 9 p.m. time of death were made.[5]

In order to bolster the case, Graham needed a witness to place Steven in the vicinity of Lawson's Bush. On Friday, June 12, he had a meeting with 13-year-old Jocelyn Gaudet, a classmate of Steven's, without her parents' presence. It's unknown what Graham said to her, according to Sher. It's not hard to imagine that the girl was intimidated by being interviewed by a police officer, but whether that influenced her recollection is not known. What is known is that her testimony at Steven's trial was instrumental in assisting the prosecution to obtain a conviction.[6]

The police also needed definitive proof of the time of death. On Friday, June 12, Cpl. Hank Sayeau took the stomach contents to a Toronto forensics lab run by the Ministry of the Attorney-General for examination. He called Graham later that day and informed him that they had the scientific proof needed to arrest Steven. In a speech in 1967, Graham told the audience: "The meal had been ingested not more than two hours prior to her death."

But Sher found contrary information. "Internal prosecution and medical documents reveal that the official written report from the laboratory — unlike the brief phone report Sayeau gave Graham — said nothing about a two-hour time limit on Lynne's death". But, for whatever reason, on Friday afternoon, June 11, Graham became convinced that Lynne died "not more than two hours" after eating supper at 5:45 – in other words, during the time she was with Steven.[7]

On Friday afternoon, Steven was returning from Bob Lawson's farm when a cruiser pulled alongside and he was told to get in. He was taken to the base guardhouse and questioned for seven hours.

In the meantime, his father, Dan Truscott, was frantically looking for him. He finally found him at the guardhouse at 11 p.m.

Graham told him he believed Steven killed Lynne. He wanted Steven examined by Dr. John Addison, a general practitioner from Clinton, and David Hall Brooks, the base medical officer. Dan Truscott and Steven reluctantly agreed, and when the doctors found lesions on his penis, they assumed the lesions could have been caused from forced penetration of an underdeveloped female.[8]

The interrogation took a bizarre turn when Graham permitted Addison to question Steven alone. I've never heard of this unorthodox tactic in my 30-year career — a doctor essentially taking on the role of criminal investigator.

When he was cross-examined at the trial by defence lawyer Frank Donnelly, Addison testified: "To the best of my knowledge, I was getting him to recall the story leading up to it... I won't say my exact words. After all, I was called out just to make a physical examination and my conversation ..."

"If you had stopped at that, I would have a lot less trouble than I have, but you didn't you see. You took on the role of a detective before you were finished," Donnelly interrupted. [9]

Steven stuck to his story, but it seemed nothing was going to change Graham's mind. It's troubling that a juvenile was questioned without his parents present. There's no doubt why Graham didn't want Steven's parents around and didn't warn him prior to taking the statement. In fact, years later at a police convention, Graham spoke about his well-planned strategy:

> "I was well aware of the judge's guidelines, that it is
> preferable to have a parent or social worker present
> when you are questioning a juvenile," he explained
> to his appreciative audience. "I was also well aware
> that it would be an exercise in futility, so I chose to
> disregard those guides."[10]

Graham's decision to disregard the legalese caused Justice Ferguson to disallow the statement at the trial.[11]

On June 13 at 3 a.m., Steven was officially arrested. The grounds were Gaudet's statement, which included an allegation that Steven arranged a date with her, the time of death established by Dr. Penistan and (supposedly) confirmed at the attorney general's lab, the lesions on Steven's penis, and a pair of red jeans he wore the evening Lynne was murdered. The jeans were seized, after police found them on a clothes line in the basement. They presumed Steven's mom washed them to destroy trace evidence. Steven was taken before a justice of the peace and formally charged. With that, his carefree life was gone and he was in a fight for his life.[12]

On July 13, 1959, Steven appeared at a preliminary hearing before Magistrate Dudley Holmes, in Goderich. A preliminary hearing is held to determine if there's sufficient evidence to put an accused on trial. After hearing 31 witnesses and examining 21 pieces of evidence, Holmes declared: "In my opinion, the evidence is sufficient to put the accused on trial and he will be committed for trial, in accordance with the Criminal Code in the form thereof."[13]

The trial began on September 16, 1959, at the County Court House in Goderich. Steven was represented by Frank Donnelly and the prosecution was lead by Glenn Hays. Robert I. Ferguson was the presiding justice. The trial lasted two weeks and 70 witnesses testified. In *Who Killed Lynne Harper?* , a 1979 book by Bill Trent and Steven Truscott, Steven recalled his thoughts regarding the trial: "As the trial progressed, however, my adolescent optimism began to fade… I realized that it had been a complete farce from the start."[14]

Steven was particularly incensed at the testimony from his friend Arnold "Butch" George. George had given the police four different versions of what he supposedly witnessed on the evening Lynne was murdered. Here are segments of the statements he gave the police, according to Julian Sher:

> Tuesday night, Butch was telling anyone who
> would listen he saw Steve take Lynne into the
> [Lawson's] Bush.

Wednesday night, Butch denied spreading that tale in front of the same boys.

By Thursday morning, Butch told the police he saw Steven and Lynne but not in the bush. This time he said he saw Lynne and Steven on the bicycle going toward the highway, after they crossed the river.

By Monday, he dramatically altered his story and told the police he had in fact not seen Steven or Lynne at all that evening, either at the bush or at the bridge until he dropped by Steve's house around 9 p.m.[15]

How could the prosecution put George on the stand? Surely, prosecutor Hays must have questioned his credibility.

Joceyln Gaudet testified Steven made a date with her to go to Lawson's Bush on Tuesday at 6 p.m. to look for newborn calves. She said Steven told her several times on the previous Monday to keep their meeting secret because the owner, Bob Lawson, didn't want kids on his property. She testified Steven came to her residence at 5:50 p.m. and asked her if they had any homework. She told him they had an English test the next day and she couldn't keep the date because she was having supper. However, she testified she did leave her residence at "about twenty after six or six thirty." She biked along the county road "to see if Steven was at the meeting place" (a tractor trail entrance) and when she didn't find him, she walked towards Lawson's Bush, "around three quarters of the way in," calling his name, but didn't see him. She then returned to the county road where she met Arnold George at the entrance to the tractor trail and they walked to the bridge. She testified she stayed at the bridge for "five or 10 minutes and then I went back to Bob's farm," but she didn't see Steven there or anywhere else that evening.[16]

Lawson's Bush where Lynne's body was found.

According to Sher, Gaudet's statement gave the authorities the motivation for the Harper homicide: Gaudet couldn't make the date, so Lynne Harper was the alternative choice to be his victim.

Bob Lawson testified that Gaudet was at his farm on June 9 at approximately ten or a quarter after seven in the evening and was there for a few minutes around the barn when he was doing chores. She was looking for Steven and was going to go back into the bush… and it was about 7:25 when she left. According to Lawson, she returned about "20 minutes or half an hour [later]."[17]

Steven was incensed at Gaudet's testimony, and in *Who Killed Lynne Harper?*, said: "Then the Crown called what it considered its key witness, a thirteen-year-old girl named Joceylne Goddette [sic] who was also in my class and her testimony really infuriated me. She testified that early on the day of the murder, I had made a date with her to look for newborn calves in Lawson's Bush. She said further, that between five thirty and six that day, I had gone to her house to collect her but not having had supper she was unable to accompany me. She was saying that I wanted to go to the very place where they found Lynne Harper. And at the time she placed me at her house,

I was actually buying coffee for my mother. How could she? I was asking the same questions I had asked about Butch George."[18]

The physical evidence the authorities used to arrest Steven was introduced at trial and rebutted by defense counsel Donnelly:

- The time of death:

    And you heard about his (Penistan's) examination. The stomach was emptied into this quart sealer and then he and Doctor Brooks took the sealer and turned it and like this and looked at it. And they say they saw this and they saw that. Now, what in the world kind of examination is that on the contents of the stomach to base a time of death? To give evidence on a serious charge such as this? Here was a government pathologist making his examination by looking at the contents in a bottle with the light against him and the light behind him. ... Now you heard the evidence of Doctor Brown. ... He specialized in disease of the stomach. And what did he tell you? He said that the stomach normally empties in between three and a half and four and a half hours, not one to two hours as Doctor Penistan said.[19]

- The red pants:

    So I suggest Mrs. Truscott was correct when she said that the other clothes were hanging on the drying line in the cellar of the Truscott home. My friend may say the fact that, you could have to find a guilty knowledge on the part of Mrs. Truscott and this boy had been implicated in the same offence. She knew nothing of it at the time. The first she knew of it was sometime in the early morning before the children had gone to school and Mr. Harper came over and she didn't even know him. She had to ask him who he was. I suggest to you that there is not a tittle of evidence to suggest any

guilty knowledge on the part of Mrs. Truscott, or
to indicate that she washed the clothes to destroy
any evidence.[20]

- Lesions on Steven's penis:

> But he [Dr. David Brooks] mentioned masturbation,
> so it is quite clear both from the evidence of Doctor
> Brooks and Doctor Addison that friction in a knot
> hole, masturbation, nothing else. That lesions could
> be caused by masturbation, nothing else … but I
> do ask you to find that the evidence is not only
> consistent, but conclusive with those lesions caused
> by masturbation. This is the opinion of Doctor
> Brown. That is the conclusion that should be drawn
> from the evidence of Doctor Addison, when he says
> it was a brush burn and it may have been caused by
> an oval shaped opening sufficiently rough to cause
> friction or wear.[21]

The jury comprised of men from Huron County had a momen-
tous task, weighing the evidence and determining guilt or innocence.
When the last witness was heard, Justice Ferguson charged the
jury. He accepted testimony of Dougie Oates and Gordon Logan,
who testified they saw Steven and Lynne pass them on the bridge,
heading towards Highway 8. But then Ferguson added: "And if
he (Truscott) had returned from the north (Highway 8), wouldn't
Jocelyne Goddette [sic] have seen him or wouldn't Arnold George
have seen him, two people who were down there looking for him."

But Ferguson's closing statement sealed Steven's fate:

> But as I pointed out to you, you must reject that
> story that he went to Number 8 Highway and the
> girl got in the car then, you must reject that story
> to convict him. If you find that although he went to
> Number 8 Highway with the girl and he brought
> her back again (and she was back, somebody
> brought her back) you will have to find that he did

bring her back again. Then the going back and forth across the bridge is of very little importance — very little importance because the question is: did he kill her? That is the point in this case.[22]

(Steven's lawyers were quick to object to Ferguson's biased pronouncement, but to no avail.)

It's one thing for a jury to hear a prosecutor or defence lawyer utter strong, seemingly slanted statements because the jury knows what "side" each is on. But it's something else to hear such words from a judge who is supposed to be impartial, with no vested interest in the outcome. Did the justice's elevated position give his words extra weight for the jury? It's impossible to know.

But it didn't take the jury members long to render a decision. In just 10 minutes, at 10:55 p.m., they returned a verdict of "guilty" with a recommendation for mercy. Judge Ferguson rendered his lethal decision:

> Steven Murray Truscott, I have no alternative but
> to pass the following sentence upon you. The jury
> have found you guilty after a fair trial. The sentence
> of this court upon you is that you be taken from
> here to the place from whence you came and there
> be kept in close confinement until Tuesday, the 8th
> day of December, 1959 and upon that day and date,
> you be taken to the place of execution and that you
> there be hanged by the neck until you are dead. And
> may the Lord have mercy upon your soul.[23]

In less than four months, the Truscotts had gone from having a normal, relatively uneventful life, to hearing their 14-year-old boy sentenced to death. Steven was incarcerated in a four-by eight-foot cell at the county jail in Goderich waiting for the day he was to die. But on the last day of November, just nine days before the scheduled hanging a guard handed him a newspaper announcing the postponement of his execution until February 16, 1960, so the Ontario Court of Appeal could consider the merits of the case.

The appeal began January 12 and lasted three days. In *The Trial of Steven Truscott*, Isabel LeBourdais named the grounds for the appeal:

> The evidence was as consistent with innocence as
> with guilt, the prosecution prejudiced the jury by
> referring to a statement signed by Steven which was
> ruled inadmissible, and the judge should have told
> the jury that even if they did not believe the defence,
> it was sufficient, if the evidence as a whole created a
> reasonable doubt.[24]

On January 20, Steven and his family were advised the appeal had been dismissed. It was a bitter disappointment except for one addendum to the ruling: his death sentence was commuted to life imprisonment.

On February 2, 1960, Steven was transferred to Kingston Penitentiary for processing and the following day, he was incarcerated at the Ontario Training School for Boys in Guelph. He remained there until his 18th birthday, when he was transferred to Collins Bay Penitentiary in Kingston, a high/medium security prison. Steven knew unless he was paroled or had his sentence overturned, the cement fortress could be his home until he died. (However, in the sixties, there was a major change in terms of rehabilitation and reintegration and Collin's Bay designed a gradual release program, which allowed inmates to work outside the institution and return in the evening.)

In April 1966 Steven received promising news, when Lester Pearson's Liberal party ordered a review by the Supreme Court of Canada. To a large extent, the impetus for this decision was the result of the tireless work of Isabel LeBourdais, a lawyer from Toronto incensed at what appeared to be a gross injustice. Her book on the case was published in March 1966 and set off an international firestorm, which ultimately put pressure on the federal government to act. Julian Sher commented on LeBourdais' courage and insight:

Her book exposed for the first time some of the glaring problems with Steve's conviction: the constantly changing stories of Butch

George, the improbabilities' in Jocelyn's tales, the contradiction in the medical testing, the dubious police tactics and the bias of the presiding judge … and the prejudices some of the jurors felt toward Steven. … Perhaps the mood of the twelve men from Huron County was best summed up by the angry words of the juror who admitted, "I knew by the third day no one was going to prove that young monster innocent. If we'd had to stay there all winter to convict that fiend, I'd have stayed."[25]

After LeBourdais' book was released, Graham, who was now assistant commissioner in charge of the Special Services division of the OPP, assigned officers from the Criminal Investigation Bureau to review his investigation. In *OPP: The history of the Ontario Provincial Police*, published in 1984, author Dahn. D. Higley (a retired member of the Criminal Investigation Bureau) included the notion that the officers assigned to review Graham's investigation believed he conducted a proper investigation and arrested the right person for the homicide.[26]

(One would think investigators outside the OPP organization should have been selected to ensure an objective investigation.)

In October 1966, the Supreme Court of Canada's nine justices heard Steven's appeal. He was represented by Arthur Martin. There were 30 witnesses, including Steven. Unfortunately, the court upheld the conviction. The justices concluded: "There were many incredibility's inherent in the evidence given by Truscott before us and we do not believe his testimony."

The lone dissenter, Justice Emmett Hall, said:

> Having considered the case fully, I believe that the conviction should be quashed and a new trial directed. … I take the view that the trial was not conducted according to law. Even the guiltiest criminal must be tried according to law. … That does not mean that I consider Truscott guilty or innocent. … The determination of guilt or innocence was a matter for the jury and for the jury alone, as its dominant function following a trial conducted according to law.[27]

This was Steven's last opportunity to prove his innocence, and he was incarcerated until October 21, 1969, when he was released on parole after serving 10 years. He moved to Guelph and with his long time advocate and partner, Marlene raised three children, Leslie, Ryan and Devon.

Steven had learned a trade in prison and worked as a millwright for a company in Guelph for seventeen years. When that plant closed, he found another job. His family never hid the fact their name was Truscott if questioned. However, for the sake of the children, they changed their name, and all corresponding government documents were in an assumed name.

In 1997, Steven had a visit from James Lockyer, a lawyer from Toronto. They went for a long walk and discussed the possibility DNA might absolve Steven of Lynne's murder. Lockyer was a founding member of the Association In Defence of the Wrongly Convicted. Their walk became a marathon and Steven and Lockyer would not cross the finish line until 2007, nearly fifty years after his initial conviction. On August 28, in a landmark ruling, the Ontario Court of Appeal quashed the conviction and Steven was acquitted of the murder of Lynne Harper. The court ruled that the "fresh evidence," if presented at a "hypothetical new trial," would significantly undermine the crown's case. The evidence included: the time of Lynne's death, Steven's location on the evening of Lynne's disappearance, Steven's post offence conduct and the evidence of lesions on Truscott's penis. The decision made headlines from coast to coast. Like many people in the rest of the country, I had followed the case and was pleased this injustice had finally been rectified.

However, I remembered that wasn't my belief in 1966 when LeBourdais' book was released. I recall reading an article on the Harper case in the now defunct *Toronto Star Weekly*. One of my reservations then was that I didn't believe Truscott could have seen something yellow on the rear of the vehicle Lynne supposedly got into from a distance of 400 metres. I told my wife then that we had the right guy, even though I knew very little about the case. I believed that Harold Graham had caught the real killer.

In a sense, this marginal knowledge and tunnel vision has helped me understand why some officers believed Truscott was guilty. However, unlike many of my former colleagues, I've now concluded Graham's rush to judgment was instrumental in convicting an innocent 14-year-old boy for the murder of Lynne Harper.

The gravesite at Union Ontario where Lynne is interred.

CHAPTER 3

PRIME SUSPECT

In the fall of 1967, I was transferred from Expo 67 in Montreal to Kitchener. The city has an interesting history and prior to the outbreak of the First World War was called Berlin. That was changed to Kitchener in 1916 as a result of anti-German sentiment. It was named in honor of Brigadier General Horatio Herbert Kitchener, who fought in the Boer War.

During the early industrial age, there was plenty of opportunity for employment at companies such as Kaufman Rubber, Electrohome, Budd Automotive and Schneider Meats. Kaufman Rubber, under the leadership of founder A.R. Kaufman, supplied contraceptives to women during the Depression. Kaufman was also one of the first industrialists to fight for women's rights in Canada.

I thought this was going to be an interesting place to work, and I wasn't wrong.

Kitchener was a busy detachment because it is in the "golden triangle," which includes Waterloo, Preston and Galt. The detachment is responsible for North Dumfries, Wilmot and Woolwich townships, as well as Highway 401. When I started, there was a staff sergeant, five corporals and 44 officers stationed at the detachment.

Provincial Constable Barry Ruhl, Kitchener OPP -1970

Const. Barry Ruhl, stationed at Kitchener, 1970.

Except for the residual trauma caused by Larry Talbot's invasion of our cottage in 1971, I was enjoying Kitchener. But life improved immensely when Pat and I were married on May 13, 1972. We rented an apartment in Waterloo and enjoyed a panoramic view of the rural countryside north of the city. We liked going for country drives in the areas populated by Mennonites, from whom we often bought fresh produce. "No Sunday Sales" signs greeted us when we approached their farms to purchase summer sausage, sauerkraut, eggs and vegetables. When our shopping was finished, we often stopped at the pub in Heidelberg to dine on succulent pigtails, sauerkraut and draft beer.

We were very busy during this period. In addition to my job, I was training for a marathon and attending the University of Waterloo in pursuit of a BA in Sociology. Pat was employed at a large law firm in Waterloo. Things were good.

But then, in the fall of 1973, Talbot entered our lives again. That September, I received a call from an Oakville Police (Halton Regional) detective who was investigating the homicide of 17-year-old Pauline Ivy Dudley. He told me Larry Talbot was the prime suspect.

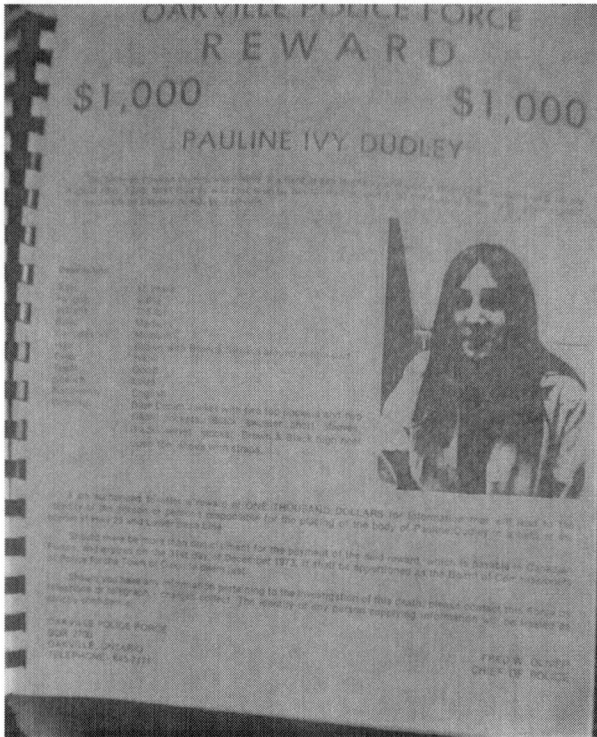

The circular distributed by the Oakville Police Department.

Pauline was last seen hitchhiking on August 10, 1973, after leaving her mother's residence on Lakeshore Boulevard in Oakville. She was going to RR 1 Milton, where she lived with her boyfriend. On August 28, her body was discovered by a farmer in a field at the corner of Lower Base Line Road and Highway 25. (Halton Regional Case 10886-73.)[1]

I asked the detective why Talbot was suspected. He said an officer on patrol had spotted an unoccupied vehicle around midnight on August 10 at a park north of Oakville, roughly a mile from where

Dudley's body was subsequently found. It was a 1973 Pontiac four-door, licence plate number 140-447, registered to Larry G. Talbot of Scarborough.

Oakville officers investigating the murder wondered if the car might be connected, went to Talbot's residence, and searched the car. In the front seat, they discovered a small spot of blood on the back of the driver's headrest and on the floor in the rear compartment they found hair, along with one strand caught in the molding. A subsequent forensic examination concluded the hair displayed characteristics similar to Dudley's, but in those pre-DNA days that was the best they could say.

When the trunk was searched, investigators discovered a "rape kit," including a wooden dildo, a jar of Vaseline, surgical tape, two well-used flashlights, two ground sheets, rope, and a couple of very sharp hunting knives. They also seized a pair of men's pants containing a minute quantity of blood, and a T-shirt with a pair of surgical gloves stuffed in the breast pocket. The officers photographed the trunk's contents and commented on its tidiness.

The officer had called me because he saw my name attached to another case involving Talbot — the cottage invasion — but other than being personally upsetting, his call was just another piece of routine business. I supplied him with whatever information I had on Talbot.

I told Pat about the call, and she said she simply wanted Talbot to disappear from her mind.

We both still felt the effects of that traumatic night in Sauble Beach, but perhaps Pat more than me. She insisted I leave the hall light on when I worked midnights.

Pat's parents owned an island northeast of Huntsville. It was a pristine playground with two cottages, two sand beaches, and a variety of vegetation, including magnificent white pines and clumps of white birch. The main cottage was built using trees from the island. The original owner also built a cottage at the opposite end of the island, facing west, so guests could watch the magnificent sunsets.

We have many fond memories of the island, including our son's initial visit at three months. We have a picture of Jeff sitting beside a cedar sapling with a big smile on his face. The cottage was an escape from our hectic lifestyles. During the day, we'd bask in the sun, swim in the cool clear lake and hike in the forest on the mainland. On rainy days, we'd relax and read in front of a crackling fire, listening to the rain on the roof.

But following the Sauble Beach break-in, we never felt totally secure, even on the island. Talbot's cottage was only 40 kilometres from us, and I kept a rifle under the bed, fearing he might discover our place on the island. This was probably paranoia, but I was ready just in case.

One night I was awakened by Pat screaming: "Barry, there's a man at the window!" I sat up, but I couldn't think. It was like I was frozen. My heart was pounding. I couldn't look out the window, fearing I'd see a masked Larry Talbot staring back at me. We never found any evidence of an intruder and concluded Pat must have had a nightmare. But it reinforced just how much Talbot still weighed on our minds.

The following year Pat went to the island with Jeff and our dog, Golden, but she lasted only one night. She went to bed and was almost asleep when she thought she heard someone attempting to break in. To add to her terror, Golden began to growl. Pat and Jeff hid in the bedroom and eventually the noise subsided. They came back the next day, though I suspect it was probably raccoons.

I wasn't immune to these scary episodes, either. Years later, after I was promoted and living in Barrie, I awoke from a terrifying nightmare of Talbot jumping out of a laundry basket, wearing a grotesque mask, pointing a gun and screaming. We both wondered if Talbot would ever leave our lives for good.

In 1978, I was assigned to the Six District Criminal Investigation Squad (CIS). This unit was, to a large extent, the brainchild of Don Westover, the detective sergeant responsible for criminal investigations in the Mount Forest district. The officers on the squad were all very experienced members selected from detachments in the district. The squad's mandate was to assist district detachments requiring additional expertise in serious criminal investigations. (I also acted as an undercover officer at Sauble Beach.)

Barry Ruhl working undercover.

I was also chosen to be the district intelligence co-ordinator (DIC) responsible for collecting, analyzing and disseminating criminal information. I attended the Canadian Police College in Ottawa in February 1978 for training. This was an intense eight-day course, and I placed fourth in the class, while Larry Edgar, also a member of the OPP, placed first. We worked on the same platoon in Kitchener in the early 1970s and, years later, would be one of the senior officers I asked to consider Larry Talbot a suspect in the Lynne Harper murder.

Although I enjoyed my career and the type of work I was perform-ing, I decided to enter the Corporal competition, and on August 1, 1979, was successful and transferred to Barrie District Headquarters. I was assigned to the crime unit, which was responsible for super-vising major criminal investigations in the district and overseeing the newly formed Seven District Criminal Investigation Squad.

There were 10 detachments in the district, from Shelburne in the south, to Huntsville in the north. One of the busiest was Wasaga Beach, which was the location of my first assignment, on Civic Holiday Weekend at the beginning of August. I was responsible for overseeing enforcement activities at the beach and employed 10 crime squad members, who performed the same role I had at Sauble Beach. (The eight male and two female officers, wore either jeans or bathing suits and walked the beach.) This strategy proved to be very effective. We managed to seize a large amount of alcohol and the beach was reasonably quiet during the weekend.

I was very busy in my new role and hadn't thought too much about Larry Talbot, but that was about to change.

CHAPTER 4

THE EPIPHANY

On July 21, 1981, a young girl in a cottage at Wasaga Beach was abducted in the middle of the night and taken to a nearby vehicle, where she was sexually assaulted. I was assigned to supervise the investigation and met with the investigating officer. As I approached the rear door of the cottage, I had a feeling of déjà vu when I spotted a rock propped up against the door to keep it ajar. Larry Talbot used the same method when he broke into our cottage. Was this a coincidence, or was it Talbot's handiwork? (On July 31, I was advised that tests conducted by the Centre of Forensic Sciences eliminated Talbot as a suspect in this assault.)

I contacted the Sauble Beach OPP detachment to see if Talbot was still active in their area. Coincidentally, Talbot had been arrested just the night before when he was observed by an officer running into the bush near King Edward Drive, and attempting to discard a pair of leather gloves as he fled. He didn't have any identification and his vehicle was discovered at an unoccupied cottage nearby. He admitted stealing lawn chairs and a table and showed the officer where he had stashed the property. When his vehicle was searched, several knives and two pairs of unlined gloves were found in the trunk.

I then contacted Halton Regional Police to ascertain if Talbot was still the prime suspect in the Pauline Ivy Dudley homicide. I was advised he was, but apparently there wasn't enough evidence to indict him. Unfortunately, DNA testing did not exist at that time as a tool for law enforcement. I recalled my conversation with the investigating officer in 1973 but it was somewhat vague, and I asked him to send me the report(s) he'd accumulated on the Dudley homicide.

On July 30, 1981 I received the correspondence as well as a memo that included the following: "An extensive investigation was conducted into him (Talbot) including polygraph, forensic work etc. but with negative results (Including surveillance.) We still strongly believe he is the man responsible."[1]

The correspondence revealed:
- Talbot's vehicle was parked a mile from the location where Pauline Dudley's body was discovered two weeks later.
- In a signed statement, Talbot admitted to being in the location where his vehicle was parked with no reason to be there.
- Hair similar to Dudley's was found on the rear compartment floor of his vehicle.
- A strand of hair similar to Dudley's was caught in a moulding in the rear compartment.
- There was a small smudge of blood on the back of the driver's headrest.
- There were small specks of blood on a pair of pants in the trunk.
- The polygraph examiner concluded Talbot's response to a number of questions was indicative of deception.
- Talbot carried a rape kit in his trunk, including an artificial penis, a jar of Vaseline, a tube of desensitizing cream, surgical gloves in the pocket of a brown T-shirt, binoculars, pair of work gloves, hockey laces, a hunting knife in a sheath, surgical tape, plastic rain coat, two ground sheets and a roll of wire.

When I read the material, I had an epiphany. If he really had killed Pauline Dudley, was she the only victim or were there others? Could he be responsible for any of the cold cases in Ontario preceding the Dudley homicide, or following it? Could Larry Talbot be a serial killer? Might he have killed Pat if she had been alone at the cottage? I didn't know the answer, but I did know that he also had a knife and four sets of hockey laces with him that night. Why? If his fantasy was to victimize women, he certainly had the tools to make it a reality, and to gain and maintain complete control over them.

In *Serial Killers*, the author Peter Vronksky defined a control-oriented murderer, and I wondered if this was the motivating factor possessed by Larry Talbot, if he was a serial killer:

> The gratification for the control-oriented murderer comes from having power over the victims, especially the "thrill" of deciding whether a person will live or die, and how and when. If a sexual assault occurs, the primary motive is achieving complete control.[2]

Larry Talbot was a travelling salesman with clientele throughout Ontario. If Pauline Dudley was offered a ride by Talbot, there would not likely have been any outward signs to set off alarm bells. When he appeared in court to answer to the charges relevant to our break-in, he was well-groomed, wearing a business suit, and had an engaging smile. He looked like a typical middle-aged businessman.

Larry Talbot in business attire attending court in Southampton

I now believe this Jekyll and Hyde character was responsible for Dudley's death. The most likely scenario is as follows:

Talbot was returning from a business trip to Buffalo and wasn't in any hurry to return home because his family was at the cottage. He spotted the young girl hitch-hiking on Lakeshore Road in Oakville and offered her a ride. Curiously, it was on a Tuesday, around the same time Lynne Harper was picked up. Pauline probably told him she was going to her residence in the Milton area. At some point, Talbot left the highway and headed for a secluded location. It's even possible he was familiar with the area. He travelled along some secondary roadways and eventually reached the secluded park. He backed the vehicle into an area surrounded by thick vegetation. Then he pulled the undoubtedly frightened and struggling girl from the vehicle, dragging her into the dense bush, during which the heel of her shoe broke off. He assaulted her for an undetermined length of time but during the attack, a cop patrolling in the area spotted his vehicle and checked it.

Talbot probably heard a vehicle door open and close as the officer checked the unoccupied vehicle. If Talbot thought it was a cop, he was probably concerned a registration check would reveal he was the owner. He waited until the officer left, then took Dudley's body from the bush and put her in a farmer's field within a mile of the site of the attack, covering her with pine branches and grass. In all probability, he didn't want to leave the body in the vicinity of where he had parked his vehicle. But he also didn't want to run the risk of being stopped or seen with her body in the vehicle, so he dumped her rather quickly and returned to his residence in Burlington, 15 minutes from the crime scene.

After reviewing all the material in the Dudley file from the Halton Regional Police, I went for a run. It was my way of dealing with stress, and after reading the report I was stressed. Generally I would relax a few minutes into a run, but it didn't happen this time. I was troubled, and my thoughts kept returning to the possibility that Larry Talbot might be a serial killer. I had personally experienced his violent side when he struck me with the gun. His occupation as a travelling salesman gave him the opportunity to prey on women in a wide area, and it also permitted him to distance himself from a crime scene.

In "A Serial Murder Symposium" sponsored by the FBI, there was a consensus that "serial murderers" are difficult to apprehend:

> For the most part, serial murder involves strangers
> with no visible relationship between the offender
> and the victim. This distinguishes a serial murder
> investigation as a more nebulous undertaking than
> that of the other crimes. Since the investigators
> generally lack an obvious connection between
> the offender and the victim, investigators instead
> attempt to discern the motivation behind the
> murder, as a way to narrow the investigative focus.[3]

The run became an uncomfortable walk as I thought about Talbot. There were too many "coincidences," but so many unanswered questions. Bottom line, could we risk leaving this guy alone? In my mind, the answer was a resounding no. We needed to monitor his activities. I decided to alert the OPP command staff about my thoughts regarding Talbot.

On August 7, 1981, I started a report on Talbot with the hope that a surveillance unit would be assigned to watch him, and maybe catch him attempting to commit an assault. It also was going to include his personal information, criminal convictions and suspected criminal activity, including the Pauline Ivy Dudley homicide. The report was also going to include the Jacqueline English homicide which occurred on October 4th, 1969, and the murder of 16 year old Suzanne Aldsworth, who was beaten to death near the village of St. Agatha, west of Waterloo, on November 17, 1972. Aldsworth left a hotel to make a phone call and her body was discovered in a ditch along a country road near St. Agatha. Talbot worked for a company with customers in the Kitchener Waterloo and London areas. On September 18, I was talking to Det. Insp. Jack Donaldson of the Criminal Investigation Bureau, who was visiting headquarters on another matter. I mentioned Talbot and my suspicion that he could be a serial killer. Donaldson was investigating the murder of 20-year-old Micheline St. Amour on July 10, 1980. St. Amour, a resident of North Bay, was found by her boyfriend and had been stabbed to death.

When I was gathering intelligence on Talbot, my contact at a credit card company found two possibly significant transactions: On November 24, 1981, a gasoline purchase at Martin River, just north of North Bay signed by L. Talbot for the vehicle registered to his company. The second was for motel accommodations in Timmins on November 26, 1981. Although these dates certainly could not be tied to the murder, it was an indication Talbot might have customers in Northern Ontario.

Donaldson suggested I send the report to him and he would include Talbot in his investigation as a "person of interest." On

January 29, 1982, I sent the report to General Headquarters for his attention.[4]

On June 11, 1982, I met with Det. Sgt. Barry Browning, my supervisor in the Barrie District Crime Unit. I hadn't heard from Donaldson or anyone from General Headquarters and thought a follow up call might assist in obtaining surveillance. Browning didn't feel there was enough compelling information to persuade the brass to authorize surveillance. His decision was concerning because of the evidence suggesting Talbot might have killed Pauline Dudley, and if so, that he might kill again. But in a top down military organization like the OPP, I had no choice but to accept his decision. On October 6, 1982, I called Donaldson and learned he had ruled Talbot out because his blood type didn't match. He also told me he contacted "the brass" in the spring and was advised surveillance couldn't be authorized for an indefinite period.

Meanwhile, on June 23, 1982, I had learned of the murder of Christine Prince in the *Toronto Star*, "Police don't have 'the slightest clue' in nanny's murder" the article said. It described Christine's activities during the previous evening, when she went to the movies with a friend. She was last seen on a "westbound St. Clair streetcar about 1:30 Monday morning." It's believed she got off the car at Wychwood Avenue to walk about two blocks to 66 Pinewood Avenue, where she worked as a nanny for Emile and Josie Kruzick. Her body was discovered "in the Rouge River about 7:15 yesterday morning near the intersection of Sewell's Road and Finch Avenue in Scarborough." Christine was reported missing by the Kruzicks when she didn't get up on Monday morning.

The story stated: "Fresh tire tracks in the mud from Sewell's Road to the river led police to believe she was slain and her body dumped about 200 yards upstream from where it was found yesterday, Insp. Soplet said. Police have no suspect or motive –'not the slightest clue'– in the case Insp. Soplet said.[5] In a subsequent release, the Homicide Squad disclosed that at 9 a.m. the same morning [Prince was discovered], a wallet belonging to her was found on a gravel apron beside Highway 401 near Meadowvale Road, roughly 30 kilometres from Pinewood Avenue. An autopsy revealed the cause of death to be drowning, but she also had sustained blows to the head and had bruises and abrasions to the head, face and body. Christine was described as a while female, 5'3", 126 pounds, blue eyes, short light brown hair, fair complexion, rosy cheeks and medium build."[6]

Police scoured the isolated area and found the murder scene about 200 metres upstream from where her body was discovered on a small tract in the bush known as a lovers' lane. It was later established that Christine had been raped. It was not believed the entrance to this road could be found or seen from Sewells Road, unless a person was familiar with the road and knew precisely where and how to enter it. Although it's possible to drive a car onto the road, it's very difficult. It was concluded the killer or killers of Christine Prince knew exactly where they were going. It appeared the killer(s) had driven from Sewells Road onto the dirt road parallel to the river for a distance of about 215 metres.[7]

The location of the homicide added to my interest in the case. Talbot lived in the vicinity of the crime scene, and there were a number of similarities in the Prince and Pauline Dudley homicides, including:

- Both victims were taken to isolated wilderness areas.
- Both homicides occurred under cover of darkness.
- Both victims were beaten about the head and sexually abused.
- There was no attempt to completely conceal the bodies.

On June 25, I contacted the Homicide Squad in Toronto and spoke to an investigator assigned to the Prince case. I gave him some of the information from the report I had sent Donaldson and expressed my belief that Talbot was quite capable of committing the homicide. He requested a copy of the report, which I sent along with a memo that said: Talbot lived in the area of the Prince crime scene, both Jacqueline English and Prince were left in creeks adjacent to wilderness areas, both suffered blows to the head, both Prince and Susan Aldsworth's purses were missing, and Talbot's penchant for travelling in the early morning hours.

I didn't hear anything from the Prince investigators, so I called Sgt. Ken Cenzura, the lead investigator on September 14. He told me they hadn't ruled Talbot out and asked for any further information I could give them. On September 16, I called Cenzura and advised him I had learned from my source at a credit card company that Talbot had been at Tramps (a bar located on Bloor Street east of Kipling in Etobicoke, about 10 Kilometres south of the abduction) on June 20, 1982, on the night, or early morning, when Prince was abducted. The credit card charge was $20.72 including a $2 tip. He told me he was attending a meeting on September 17 with officers from the F.B.I., who were preparing a psychological profile on the type of individual responsible for the Prince homicide and would mention Talbot.

On September 28, I called Cenzura to see if Talbot was still a person of interest. He told me nothing else had transpired, but he was sending someone to the credit card company to get a copy of the transaction.

On September 29, I had a meeting with Det. Sgt. Browning and suggested that we should attempt to get a surveillance team to monitor Talbot's activities. He didn't think we'd be successful, but thought it might be something to consider in the future, if Metro homicide didn't investigate Talbot.

On November 9, 1982, I read about the murder of 25-year-old Delia Adriano in the *Toronto Star*.[8] Above the headline "Last hope ends for Delia's parents," I wrote: Found off Guelph line in Burlington. Talbot's home area! (The Burlington address was Talbot's previous residence. He was residing in Scarborough at the time of Adriano's homicide.)

Delia was last been seen walking towards the side entrance of her residence on Wildwood Drive in Oakville, on Sunday, September 26, 1982 at 9:30 p.m. Her boyfriend had driven her home after watching a soccer game. Subsequently, witnesses reported hearing a woman screaming in the area of Wildwood Drive and Slade Crescent and a young woman fitting Delia's description was observed being forced into a dark sub-compact vehicle by a male. A struggle continued inside the car, which left the area with the headlights turned off.

On Saturday, November 6, 1982, the naked, partly decomposed body of Delia Adriano was located in a wooded area near the 2nd Line and No. 3 Side Road in Milton, more than 30 kilometres from her home. She was discovered by a man cutting wood in an area known as a lovers' lane. He told the media he tripped and dropped his chainsaw right at her feet.[9] Delia was a graduate of Gordon E. Perdue High School in Oakville and was employed by Wear Check International of Toronto.

On November 11, 1982, I called Sergeant Ted Waller, the officer who had been involved in the Dudley homicide and was assisting the investigators in the Adriano investigation. We discussed the Adriano homicide and he said they didn't have much to go on. He said her body was in an advanced state of decomposition and the crime scene was in the same general area where Dudley had been found. They were presently in the process of checking 40 vehicles that were seen in the vicinity of the crime scene. I told him I had placed Talbot on C.P.I.C. for "observation" regarding the Dudley homicide and he said he'd advise the Adriano investigators of the entry.

On November 29, I received a call from Const. Glen Randall, regarding the Adriano homicide. He wanted to know if my credit card contact could place Talbot anywhere on September 26, the day Adriano was abducted. I advised him there was one purchase of gas in the amount of $26.67 at a B.P. station at the intersection of Young and Markham Road in Richmond Hill. I suggested he check with Adriano's relatives about any bars or restaurants she may have frequented and cross-check with the credit card company to determine if Talbot could be placed at any of the same premises. I also suggested he determine the proximity of Talbot's company to Wear Check where Delia was employed. On November 30, Randall called and told me Wear Check was only a quarter-mile from Talbot's place of employment.

On January 12, 1983, I called Randall to determine the status of the investigation and he advised me they were winding it down. And in terms of Talbot, the only connection they had was the close proximity of the companies where Talbot and Adriano were employed.

On February 3, I travelled to Toronto to determine the actual distances between Talbot's residence and the Prince crime scene, and the distance between the Talbot and Adriano's places of employment. I also met with Les Church, who had known Talbot for many years and worked with him at Industrial Plumbing during 1959-1960.

I calculated the distance from Talbot's residence in Scarborough to the bridge located on Sewells Road, where Christine's body was discovered. It took eight minutes and 51 seconds and I stopped for three traffic lights. The distance between his residence and the bridge was seven kilometres.

I then drove to Talbot's workplace and calculated the distance from there to the Wear Check where Adriano worked. It was only two kilometres. It was an interesting discovery, but was it simply a coincidence?

The closeness of their workplaces meant there was any number of ways Delia could have come to Talbot's attention. She was a very attractive woman and would stand out in a crowd. He could have spotted her when he was driving around in the vicinity of Wear Check, or he may have even visited her office or nearby businesses in the course of his work. If she was targeted, he could have followed her and discovered where she lived. If it was a crime of convenience, he simply could have spotted Delia and her boyfriend and followed them to her residence. But this was all speculation and there was no evidence pointing in any of those directions.

There are, however, a number of similarities between the Adriano and Prince homicides:

- Adriano and Prince were both 25 years old.
- Both were petite.
- Both were abducted after dark.
- Both were sexually assaulted.
- Both were left naked.
- Both were left in areas known as lovers' lanes.
- There was no effort to conceal either body.
- Both were abducted on Sunday.
- Both were transported approximately 30 kilometres.

There were also a number of similarities between these two cases and the murder of Pauline Ivy Dudley. She also was abducted after dark, sexually assaulted and left in an isolated wilderness area and there was no effort to conceal her body.

On February 3, I met with Les Church*, at his company office. Church had appeared as a character witness for Talbot at two trials (including ours) and also had helped Talbot get two different jobs. Church told me Talbot was a complete loner and that when Talbot served time at the Mimico correctional institution, no one but Church visited him. Talbot had told Church he didn't know what caused him to commit crime. He said something came over him and he wasn't in control of himself. He also said he saw a psychiatrist at the Clarke Institute but, "the guy didn't do anything for him." He also told Church his father beat him with a cane when he was a youngster.

Church said Talbot was employed by Industrial Plumbing* and Church took over the territory in January 1960. I was interested in the locations he visited and asked him to point them out on a map.[10]

Map and the location of Industrial Plumbing customers.

As he did I circled them. They included Goderich, Clinton, Mitchell, Exeter, St. Mary's, Woodstock, Wingham, Listowel, Fergus, Kincardine, Teeswater, Orangeville, Hanover, Walkerton, Owen Sound, Meaford and Collingwood. I asked Church about Clinton:

"Why did you visit Clinton, Les?"

"Oh, the Clinton Air Force Base purchased plumbing supplies from us."

Immediately, the Lynne Harper homicide came to mind.

"Les, would you remember any of the vehicles Talbot drove?"

"No, I'm not very good with cars but there's a guy, Bill Elliott,* who worked with us and he's a real car fanatic who'd probably remember."[11]

As I drove back to Barrie after the interview, I thought about what Church had said. Larry Talbot probably visited the Clinton Air Force Base from 1951 to1959. I remembered that Lynne Harper was hitch-hiking prior to the discovery of her body in Lawson's Bush. And Steven Truscott had said he saw her get into a "late model Chevrolet." I also knew Talbot was the prime suspect in the murder of Pauline Ivy Dudley, who was last seen hitch-hiking in the Oakville area. I concluded there were parallels in the cases that should be explored.

On February 4, I met with my boss, Det. Sgt. Barry Browning, and briefed him on the interview with Church, including the possibility that Talbot visited the Clinton Air Force Base in 1959. Then I suggested that maybe the OPP had arrested the wrong person for the Lynne Harper homicide.

He told me not to mention my suspicions regarding Harper in the report I was preparing for headquarters. He also mentioned the time I was spending on an investigation that didn't involve our district. He showed me a district crime sheet analysis and suggested my investigative role should be confined to the district. I left the meeting with ambivalent feelings. I could understand why the Harper-Talbot hypothesis would be a concern for Browning. There was no way he wanted to sign off on a report that included the notion Steven Truscott might not be the person responsible for the Harper homicide. In fairness to Browning, I also had believed initially that Insp. Harold Graham got the right guy and the courts had found Truscott guilty of the homicide. There was more work to be done.

When I left the meeting with Browning, I went to another office and called Les Church. This time, I taped the conversation:

BR: And [Larry] went to those areas where you [were] servicing the places we discussed yesterday at that time?

LC: Yeah.

BR: For instance Goderich at the salt mines?

LC: Right.

BR: Clinton, at the air force base?

BR: Would there be a lot of orders out of say the air force base in Clinton?

LC: Right, right

LC: No, there would not be a lot. There'd be mainly parts for boilers, stuff like that. We didn't do a lot of business at those bases but it was nice steady business. They usually came in on a tender and you could usually get a good margin on it, you know.

BR: Yeah. Like how many visits would you do to a place like that?

LC: Like, Clinton?

BR: Yeah

LC: Probably four to six a year... Like, you go probably once every two months, something in that area, you know.

BR: When you got all the customers that essentially Industrial had at the time, would you have got that from Larry that those areas were done, those specific customers, or would it have come from Industrial?

LC: It would have come from Industrial. One of the problems I had with Larry was that he would give me no information. When I first went into that territory that was a real hassle I had with him. The way I got my customer, he handed me a telephone book... And said, "Here, kid, go through the Yellow Pages." that was one of the biggest difficulties I had with that guy from the beginning.

BR: You mentioned yesterday that he said something to the effect that he said he doesn't know what comes over him?

LC: Yeah, it's the old story… I was thinking about that last night to the pitch that sort of got me hooked on it, and he used it in court to. It's sort of the well-to-do businessman, he's really not doing this for money or anything, and it's some psychological thing that comes over him in times of great stress or great pressure and causes him to revert to something from his childhood. That's the pitch I got from his lawyer and that's the pitch from Talbot and then from (when) he went to see a psychiatrist (at) the Clark Institute.

BR: Yeah, they have that facility.

LC: Yeah and I don't know if you've seen any of the reports or talked to the guy that talked to him, but he would never let me get close to any of the reports, and he claimed that the guy didn't do anything for him really.

BR: I see.

LC: Other than to tell him it was something in his past, in his childhood, something back there that anytime I've talked to him about his father he'd say mean old so and so, who had one leg and used to hit him with his crutch.

BR: I see.

LC: Nothing about his mother, didn't know his mother very well at all from what I gather.

BR: Yeah.

LC: And he used it very successfully in court. Got him off I don't know how many times. It's incredible; I can't believe our judicial system.

BR: Yeah.

LC: When a guy gets involved that many times (and) he gets off that lightly. It's incredible.

After speaking to Church, I called Bill Elliott* to see if he remembered the vehicle Talbot was driving in 1959:

BE: '58, I can tell you he had a Chevrolet two-door-210, a baby blue colour and you know there was a chrome spear over the back rear quarter that was painted white in there and had a white top cream I guess would be more exact.

BR: OK so?

BE: V8.

BE: '57 to '60 he drove that car.

BR: OK, now the '57, that's the one that had — it wasn't the cat's eyes — it had the fin. Is that's what you're saying to me?

BE: Yeah. Oh I know what you're referring to. You're looking at the back of the car.

BR: Yeah.

BE: Yeah OK. The '57 had a tail. It didn't have any uplift to it. It was parallel to the ground, it had a chrome cap on the fender that went right out to the end and cut back diagonally back towards the bumper and the taillights sort of sat just above the bumper.

BR: Just above the bumper?

BE: Yeah, I have a beautiful picture in my mind but what are you thinking — a '55 with a little tail light on?

BR: I was thinking more if he had a '58 or '59 Chev.

BE: Oh no, he never had one of those.

BR: It was definitely '57?

BE: Oh absolutely!

BR: And that was the colour like a robin's egg blue and cream top and . . .

BE: Oh yeah!

BR: OK, would it be a two- or four-door?

BE: Two-door, V8 model, 210 and that was middle of the line.

BR: In '60, is that when they changed cars?

BE: Yeah.

BR: What would he have then?

BE: He had a copper-coloured 1960 Pontiac two-door Strato Chief, which is the bottom of the line.[12]

(Talbot was interviewed on September 27, 2000 by the OPP at his residence and admitted driving a 1957 Chevrolet in 1959, as described by Bill Elliott.) I put the tapes of my conversations with Church and Elliott in a secure location and finished the report. Heeding the instruction from Browning, I did not include the Harper homicide, although I thought it would have been the responsible thing to do. I really didn't have any confidence the OPP would re-open any of the cases but in the closing remarks, I suggested a joint force strategy be considered, including the OPP, Toronto and Halton Regional Police. I concluded:

There have been a number of women who have mysteriously disappeared and others whose bodies have been discovered the victims of sexually related offences over the many past years in Ontario. In considering Talbot as perhaps the suspect in any number of these crimes I consider one significant point. He was probably involved in the Pauline Ivy Dudley homicide in 1973. Was this his first act of homicide and his last? Or was he doing others before or since that killing?

Hopefully, a concentrated effort by a Joint Force Program may answer these questions.

J.B. Ruhl, Corporal

for Detective Sergeant B.L. Browning[13]

The report was forwarded to OPP General Headquarters in Toronto on March 15, 1983 for the attention of Det. Insp. M. R. Stroud and copies were sent to the Metropolitan Toronto Police for the attention of Staff Sgts. R. Strathdee and K. Cenzura and the Halton Regional Police for the attention of Staff. Sgt. Ian Algar. I had mixed feelings about the report's content. On one hand, it contained information suggesting Talbot probably killed Pauline Dudley and might be responsible for other cold cases, including Christine Prince and Delia Adriano. But in neither of these homicides did the investigations reveal the incriminating evidence discovered in the Dudley murder. But I was disappointed the Lynne Harper homicide wasn't in the report because I thought it was significant that Larry Talbot probably visited the Clinton Air Force Base in 1959. There also were a number of similarities between the two homicides, including the fact both victims were last seen hitch-hiking.

On March 25, 1983, I was at General Headquarters and my journal notes included the following:

Was in Toronto GHQ, Nelson Kinkaid (Cpl.
Intelligence Branch) called me into his office and
told me he was just reading the report. He read off a
yellow piece of paper from George Marshall, Const.

Intelligence Branch. It said — read this, takes about
20 minutes but if we collar this guy it would be a
real feather in our hat. Later on that day at approx.
3 p.m. I went into Rod William's office. (Staff Sgt.
Intelligence Branch.) We were joined by Nelson
Kinkaid and Bob Matthews, (Cpl. Intelligence
Branch.) and Insp. Bob Patterson Intelligence
Branch (Retired Supt.). He stopped and made my
day. He congratulated me for the report. I suggested
that we should do a computer printout on sex crime
murders unsolved in the province since the '60s, he
seems receptive.[14]

On March 31, Project Tree was approved and surveillance began
on Talbot. My journal included the following:

At 9:50 am I called Nelson Kinkaid. He told me
they went up on him (commenced surveillance) this
morning. He also said that in 2 ½ years of working
for (Supt. Ron Faulhaufer, Commander-Intelligence
Branch), he had never seen him so excited about a
project-I hope he won't be disappointed.[15]

On April 8, I received a call from Nelson Kinkaid. He advised
me Const. Ron Allen was the analyst assigned to the project. He
also said he found the "segments ref. Truscott-Harper he got from
Wayne Frechette very interesting."[16] (I have no notes or recollection
regarding the specific "segments" that Kinkaid mentioned.)

Wayne Frechette was a corporal assigned to the surveillance
team and I had told him about my hypothesis regarding the possible link between Harper and Talbot. Ironically, Frechette followed
in Harold Graham's footsteps and became a Criminal Investigation
Bureau (CIB) inspector. In 1997, he was promoted to chief superintendent of the CIB and was a key player when I attempted to get
the OPP to investigate Talbot in 1997.

On April 28, I spoke to Frechette on the fifth floor at General
Headquarters. He told me the surveillance team observed Talbot

trying to help a motorist in distress but when he discovered there was a male with the female he took off.

The surveillance team also watched Talbot when he stole hubcaps from a vehicle. After speaking with Frechette, I had lunch in the cafeteria with Tom Randall, a corporal in the Intelligence Unit (who retired as superintendent at Chatham), and we were discussing Talbot when he said "The guy's a sicko and will probably end up in Penetang." (a hospital for the criminally insane in Penetang, Ont.). Randall also said "We can't afford to leave him alone now." I spoke to Nelson Kinkaid after lunch and he told me they were still on "my friend worth doing and definitely a Clepto (thief)."[17]

(In 2004, the Kaufman Inquiry reviewed the Steven Truscott conviction. It was conducted by Fred Kaufman, a former judge of the Quebec Court of Appeal. Truscott was represented at the inquiry by James Lockyer and lawyers from The Association in Defense of the Wrongly Convicted. On October 28, 2004, Justice Minister Irwin Cotler asked the Ontario Court of Appeal to review Truscott's conviction following his review of Kaufman's submission.)

I learned years later, after reviewing the Kaufman Inquiry transcripts, that in April 2004, the OPP Behavioural Science Unit (BSU), had released information at the inquiry regarding their surveillance activities on Talbot, including the fact that he frequented strip clubs in Buffalo, cruised late at night in areas known as lovers' lanes and attempted to pick up hitchhikers.[18] During Project Tree, I recall waking almost every morning and wondering if that was the day Talbot would be caught. There were many times I was tempted to contact Det. Insp. Murray Stroud, the supervisor of the project, but reasoned since I didn't hear from him, I wasn't in the loop.

Unfortunately, disaster struck on May 4 and Project Tree went south. Talbot was pulled over for speeding on Highway 11 in an area patrolled by the Orillia Detachment, and when the officer called dispatch to check Talbot on the Canadian Police Information Centre (CPIC) system for warrants, Talbot overheard the dispatcher tell the officer he (Talbot) was an "active criminal," or words to that effect. In fact, the CPIC entry for Talbot mentioned the Pauline Dudley homicide and named Talbot as the "prime suspect."

Prior to the implementation of Project Tree, I had entered Talbot's license plate on the CPIC system with the expectation that if he was prowling around on foot and an officer checked his vehicle, he'd become aware of Talbot's status on the CPIC system. This revelation would serve to alert the officer to the possibility that Talbot was involved in a criminal activity in the area and result in a search for him. The vehicle information could also be used as an investigative tool in the event Talbot wasn't located and a criminal offence had occurred.[19]

On May 9, the corporal in charge of the Communications Unit at my detachment in Barrie came to my office and wanted to know if I knew Larry Talbot. He said he'd spent the last 20 minutes with Talbot, who was upset because he was on the "computer system." Talbot told the corporal he went to General Headquarters in Toronto to complain about being in CPIC and was sent to Barrie. He said his marriage was already shaky and he had to explain to his wife, who was with him during the traffic stop, why his car was being searched. During that stop, he also overheard the dispatcher sending another cruiser to assist the officer at the scene.[20]

The response to all of this from the OPP was very disappointing and I was told the project was being scaled down. An officer whom I trust later told me Det. Insp. Murray Stroud blamed me for leaving Talbot on CPIC as a "person for observation." In fairly short order, Talbot was yesterday's news and the project was scrapped. Initially, the command staff had approved, so why the sudden change, especially in view of the officers in the Intelligence Unit, who believed he was worth watching? And during surveillance, someone at the executive level probably presumably had received updates and knew the surveillance team followed him through lovers' lanes at night and watched him attempting to pick up female hitch-hikers.

I was never given an explanation, but perhaps they felt Talbot had been tipped off by what he heard from the Orillia dispatcher and that was the rationale for cancelling the surveillance. Or, perhaps there were other reasons for cancelling the project, including the expense already incurred, pending projects requiring the immediate assistance of the surveillance team, or maybe the administration had second thoughts about my serial killer hypothesis.

In any case, Larry Talbot was now travelling throughout Ontario, free from surveillance I worried that other unsuspecting women could become his victims. But there were other things I needed to worry about, too. On October 17, 1983, Det. Sgt. Browning advised me that R.W. Burkett, the Superintendent of District Seven, wanted a written review of my work performance. He said GHQ wasn't happy with the Talbot report I had written and there were things in it that weren't factual. Browning also told me he hadn't received the report with the complaints about me, but thought I should know.

He had also received a complaint from a CIB Inspector regarding my performance at a homicide scene, and the fact that I didn't continue assisting him with the investigation. The case involved the murder of a woman in the Bradford detachment area. I was assigned to the investigation and essentially my role was to supply the inspector with whatever resources he required, as well as performing functions such as intelligence-gathering. I attended the scene on Sept. 29-30. But, I was also a member of the OPP running team and we were scheduled to compete in the Detroit Police Games on Oct. 1-2. I called Supt. Burkett at his residence on the evening of Sept. 29 and apprised him of the upcoming competition. I also advised him that Cpl. John Allan of the Bradford detachment was going to be available in my absence.

Browning told me the inspector didn't think I was "interested" in the investigation but couldn't supply me with the specific instances that led the inspector to arrive at this conclusion. I was never confronted with the alleged performance deficiencies. I have retained the comprehensive notes I made during the investigation and simply have no idea what the inspector was referencing.

When I was writing the book, I read a Personnel Evaluation Report prepared by Browning for the time period 20 Aug. 81 to 08 Sept. 82.[21] In the section entitled Assessment of Employee's Performance he had written that I was instrumental in bringing several major crimes to a successful conclusion, including Project Scam (Seize Cocaine and Marihuana), which was a major drug investigation in the Bracebridge Detachment area. It had resulted in the arrest of a large number of individuals for trafficking and assisted the Metro Police Force in seizing heroin valued slightly under $1 million.(I received a "Letter of Commendation" from Comm. H.H. Graham.) He mentioned my involvement in a surveillance of persons responsible for break-ins in the Stayner and Collingwood area, which led to several arrests and charges. He also said, "In addition, he has supervised squad activities in relation to hotel checks for LLA (liquor violations) and nudity or obscene performance investigations. In each case Corporal Ruhl's performance has been excellent."

The evaluation had been forwarded to Burkett, who had signed off on it as follows: "I concur with the contents of this report. I am aware of this member's position and it is gratifying to see that he is performing so well." Signed, R.W. Burkett, Superintendent.

I received my next evaluation for the period 08 Sept. 82 to 22 Sept. 83, 25 days before the October 17 meeting. In the Assessment of Employee's Performance, Browning said: "Corporal Ruhl's devotion to duty cannot be questioned. He is a sincere and interested member of the Force. He has been instrumental in bringing several major crimes to a successful conclusion."

"However, it appears that over the four years that he had been assigned to his present position, his efforts have been somewhat misdirected. This was included in the section outlining areas for improvement. (There was one particular investigation I supervised in the Midland detachment area we discussed. It was a robbery that occurred on July 30 when an elderly man was severely beaten. Browning was concerned with the lack of searches in the area of the crime scene. He also mentioned that I was "extremely upset" when questioned about the length of time I spent transcribing audio recordings obtained from the suspect(s) interviewed about the robbery. I apologized and Browning commented: "In all fairness, he seems to have made a conscious effort to overcome this problem, since it was brought to his attention.")

It should be noted the above comments do not reflect a sudden change in Corporal Ruhl's performance. These comments are made because the writer (Browning, referring to himself in the third person) has started only in the past short period of time, to become aware of some of the shortcomings. The writer had not had time to initiate meaningful corrective action and these comments are made for the purpose of spelling out the problem, so that a starting point can be determined to correct the problem. I have no doubt that, given the proper direction, Corporal Ruhl will make every effort and is fully capable of performing his duties properly."

The evaluation was forwarded to Supt. Burkett. who added the following comments: "I concur with the content of this report. It is anticipated that Corporal Ruhl will receive the proper direction and that he in turn will make every effort to perform his duties properly. He must also realize that we all have to be prepared to accept constructive criticism from our superiors for the betterment of the Force. R.W. Burkett, Superintendent."[22]

On October 20, 1983, I met with Supt. Burkett. It quickly became evident his comments in the evaluation report regarding me receiving "proper direction" wasn't what was actually going to happen. Burkett told me I was being transferred out of the crime unit. He said I'd lost "credibility" with the Criminal Investigation Bureau and Dep. Comm. Bill Lidstone, the Commander of Field Operations, wanted me out of the unit. He also said the OPP had spent thousands of dollars on the Talbot investigation and got nowhere. This was a disconcerting situation. Browning had told me October 17 that there were allegations of factual errors in my report on Talbot, but they were never outlined to me, I was never questioned about them, and as far as I know, they were never investigated.

CHAPTER 5

ON THE ROAD AGAIN

In January 1984, I was transferred to Barrie Detachment, which was in the same building as the District Headquarters Crime Unit, where I previously worked, and was put in charge of "A" Platoon. This was a lateral transfer, but instead of district supervision, I was responsible for a platoon deployed in the Barrie Detachment area. I was 40 years old and had been a member of the OPP for 19 years.

But before starting in my new position, I entered the Donwood Institute in Toronto for a six-week treatment program. I had quit drinking way back in 1973 and traded the booze for running shoes, with which I found a healthier way to get my highs. I made the decision to quit when I knew I was drinking to excess and believed it would eventually affect my health and my job. I'd also witnessed the negative effect it had on family members who were alcoholics, and I knew it was just a matter of time before I'd experience the same fate. But, after my transfer from the crime unit, I was extremely upset at the way the organization had treated me and I was concerned I might relapse. The Donwood was just what the doctor ordered. The time away from the organization and the support I received from the staff helped me immensely.

On the eve of returning to duty, I couldn't sleep. I was anxious because my new role was vastly different from my responsibilities in the crime unit. I was also experiencing some anxiety as I put on a uniform I hadn't worn for eight years and reported for duty. But as I entered the detachment, I was greeted with a handshake from the first officer I met.

I gradually became comfortable in my new role and the support I received from my platoon helped considerably. The officers assigned to general law enforcement duties are, to a large extent, the backbone of the organization. They're exposed to every type of occurrence from the trivial to the most tragic. And I can unequivocally say the officers I had the privilege of supervising were very capable and supportive of each other. I don't know why I was given the nickname "Dad," but that's what the platoon members called me when the brass weren't around.

Following the first year, I received a Personnel Evaluation Report for the period 22 September, 1983 to October 18, 1984,[1] prepared by Staff Sgt. L.J. Jones. In the Assessment of Performance category Jones said:

> Cpl. Ruhl came to Barrie detachment without the
> benefit of prior experience as a shift supervisor, field
> level. I have been most impressed by his energetic
> approach to his new duties. He spent many hours
> researching and as he gained necessary experience
> has become a most competent and confident super-
> visor. His subordinates and peers and supervisor
> have the utmost regard for Cpl. Ruhl. His recent
> involvement in the Papal visit was handled in a
> competent manner. Cpl. Ruhl's platoon is operating
> in an above average manner and its members have
> handled several serious occurrences and in the most
> part successfully. His preparation and submission
> of month end statistics are completed promptly
> and correctly.

The evaluation was reviewed by Insp. E.K Zalman who wrote:

> I agree with the content of this report. Corporal
> Ruhl's above-average performance in his capacity as
> shift supervisor is recognized and appreciated. His
> positive outlook has assisted him in being recom-
> mended to compete in the Corporal to Sergeant
> Process, November 84.

I was exposed to many tragedies during the period I was stationed at Barrie but there's one that stands out in the never-ending saga of man's inhumanity to man. In the early-morning hours of June 29, 1992, two men shot and killed a young man in the Bracebridge area and fled south on Highway 11 in the victim's truck. They were pulled over on Highway 400 in the Barrie Detachment area for speeding by Scott Couse, a member of my platoon. When Scott approached the vehicle he heard the driver say, "Good evening officer" and then he was shot. Scott was wearing body armour, which probably saved his life. He was rushed to the nearby hospital and, following an extended stay, recovered from his injuries.

During the days following the shooting, I assisted a psychologist in the capacity of peer support provider. We conducted a number of Critical Incident Stress Debriefings for the officers working with Scott the evening he was shot. These debriefings are conducted a short time after a traumatic event, and give officers an opportunity to share their thoughts and feelings in a secure environment.

We also held a second debriefing for the families of the officers involved. This was essentially intended to make the families aware of the effects of post traumatic stress disorder on the officers. The families also are advised of the coping mechanisms and support services available to them in the community.

It was a challenging time for personnel following the shooting and was a reality check for all of us. I remember accompanying an officer on patrol and when we pulled over a vehicle, we both approached the passenger door, when normally we'd go to the driver's door. Uptight? You bet!

Scott was an inspiration to us all. After his return to work, he attended the OPP Academy and spoke to the recruit classes about his traumatic experience and the benefits of Critical Incident Stress Debriefings. He was eventually promoted to the rank of sergeant.

I was busy in my supervisory role and didn't spend much time thinking about Larry Talbot until I read a newspaper article on Saturday, January 8, 1994. The headline in the *Toronto Star* was riveting: "Six slayings may be linked." The story went on to say: "The unsolved sex slayings of six women in southern Ontario show a number of striking similarities, suggesting the murders are linked, a Star investigation indicates."[2]

The reporters, Nick Pron and John Duncanson, included the murders of Jenny Isford, Christine Prince, Delia Adriano, Valerie Stevens, Lynda Shaw and Cindy Halliday. The cases stretched from 1982 to 1992. All the women were kidnapped and driven to remote areas, where they were sexually assaulted and murdered. All the incidents happened between early spring and late summer. (The Isford and Shaw murders have since been solved. The others are outstanding cold cases.)

Two of the investigators admitted the possibility several of the killings could be linked: "I'm impressed with the similarities . . . perhaps the cases should be seriously reviewed as a whole," said Halton Region Inspector John Van der Lelie, who investigated the Adriano case.[3]

Det. Insp. Rick Kotwa of the OPP Criminal Branch, who was investigating the Stevens slaying, added: "One thing's for sure, the killer had to know the location of that lovers' lane before taking her there. . . I'll admit I've just about run out of leads," adding "there were areas of the Star's research that might be worth pursuing."[4]

One of the victims, 17-year-old Cindy Halliday, was last seen hitchhiking on Highway 27 near the village of Midhurst on April 20, 1992. She was returning to Waverley, a village northeast of Elmvale. On June 16, 1992, her body was discovered in a reforestation area near Horseshoe Valley Road (County Road 22 and Flos Township Road 2), about 10 kilometres north of where she was picked up. At the time of this killing, Larry Talbot was living in a town one hour north of where Halliday's body was found. On July 18, 1993, Talbot was ticketed for speeding on County Road 22 by an officer on my platoon. I asked him what the guy was like. He said something to the effect he was very personable.

The *Toronto Star* article also included something I found very interesting: "Before disposing of her body, the killer had a twisted plan, investigators believe. He left her neatly folded coat near a road and later, more than a week after it was discovered and police had searched the area, he returned to drop off her dismembered body."[5]

This behaviour was somewhat similar to evidence found at the Lynne Harper homicide. Her clothes were also neatly arranged. And in that case, the killer may have taunted the police by placing a heart-shaped gold locket Lynne had been wearing on a fence wire near the road, so it would be found. This was referenced by Isabel LeBourdais in *The Trial of Steven Truscott*:

On June 19, ten days after Lynne disappeared, and six days after Steven was arrested . . . Sandra Archibald was picking berries on the edge of Lawson's Bush by the County Road when she found a heart-shaped gold locket with the R.C.A.F. crest on it hanging over the lowest wire of the somewhat dilapidated barbed wire fence, just as if someone had tossed it from a passing car. . . . Police had searched the Bush and they had also paid particular attention to the fence, looking for signs that a girl or bicycle had been pulled through. It was a reasonable inference that the murderer might have returned some days after the crime and either tossed or placed the locket on the wire of the fence right by the road, so that it would be found.[6]

> The *Toronto Star* article mentioned a theory adopted by the Federal Bureau of Investigation that "leaving clues may be a form of taunting. As a killer eludes capture he may grow bolder, showing a trait known as 'invincibility and invisibility' — the notion that he can never be caught."[7]

I read the Star article a number of times and decided once again to put pen to paper and contact the OPP Criminal Investigation Bureau. On January 14, 1994, I sent a report to Det. Insp. Barry Thompson, lead investigator in the Halliday homicide, and included a copy of the report that had been instrumental in persuading the brass to implement Project Tree.

The correspondence included the fact that Talbot lived about an hour north of where Halliday's body was discovered. I also mentioned the speeding ticket he received on July 8, 1983, on County Road 22, which proved that he travelled that road. "In reviewing the report, I still believe Talbot should be considered a suspect in the homicides and an effort made to either eliminate or indict him," I wrote.[8]

I was never contacted by Insp. Thompson, but when I was talking to my next door neighbour on September 24, 1994, he told me he was at a party with Chief Supt. Wayne Frechette, who wanted me to know he was investigating Talbot for the Cindy Halliday homicide. He also told my neighbour he deployed two "hitchhikers" but wasn't successful. I assume he meant two female police officers working undercover, who attempted to entice Talbot to pick them up.

What a difference 10 years and a change in command staff had made. A decade after Project Tree was scrapped, Talbot was once again a "person of interest." However, I was not privy to the ongoing investigation into the Halliday murder and I can only guess that no links to Talbot were found.

By now I was 50 years old, and was anxiously awaiting my retirement as a uniformed cop and the start of a new career as an addiction counsellor with the OPP. Several months earlier, I'd approached the OPP psychologist and convinced him an addiction counsellor was required in the organization and the OPP Command Staff had agreed. But it was an anxious time. My retirement date was still several months away and I was still supervising a shift and responding to calls when the platoon was short of personnel. I remember reading about a cop who was within hours of retiring from the New York Police Department when he was shot and killed. I decided to team up with a member of the platoon during the afternoon shifts and it helped to alleviate the anxiety I occasionally experienced.

Those final months were not without incident. One day I was driving through Midhurst, a usually peaceful village eight kilometres north of Barrie, when the communications unit sent me to an abandoned vehicle occurrence on St. Vincent Street near Willow Creek. When I arrived at the scene, I requested a check on the licence plate to ascertain who the owner was. There wasn't anyone near the vehicle, and I was about to search the area when the dispatcher asked me to call him from a telephone, because our cruiser radios were monitored by the public. I was living in Midhurst in those pre-cell-phone days so I went home and called from there. The dispatcher told me he had received a call from a person who worked with a physiotherapist at a Barrie clinic who hadn't come to work that morning. Her residence was located on Finlay Mill Road, a short distance from my home.

I arrived at the residence and met the man who had called us. He was in severe shock. He had entered the house looking for his friend and found her lifeless body in the basement.

I entered the home through the side door and started down the steps to the basement, where I saw a horrific sight. The woman was propped up against the clothes dryer. She had been shot in the head and sustained multiple stab wounds.

The investigation revealed that a 21-year-old man who was a client at the clinic had been infatuated with the young woman, to the extent that he gave her a mountain bike the week before he murdered her. The abandoned vehicle on St. Vincent Street was his. He had walked into Willow Creek and committed suicide, shooting himself in the head.

I remember going home that evening and painting the basement walls white.

CHAPTER 6

RETIRED AND REHIRED

In April, 1994, I retired from the OPP after 30 years. I had spent a rewarding career in an organization second to none. In 1964, I had appeared before an oral board and was asked why I wanted to become a police officer. I replied, "I wanted to help people." Now I was entering a new career as a civilian, but still helping people, specifically OPP officers and their families experiencing substance abuse issues. (In 1994, I completed a practicum at the Donwood Institute in Toronto to satisfy York University's requirements for the Bachelor of Social Work (Hons) degree. It was the ideal placement to train for a career in the addiction field.)

I was employed by the OPP as an addiction counsellor for the next four years and really enjoyed the challenge of helping folks help themselves. I also assisted the force psychologist in responding to traumatic events requiring Critical Incident Stress Debriefings for OPP personnel. There was one dreadful incident that stood out among the many I attended. On May 31, 1997, Tom Coffin, a 32-year-old constable at Midland Detachment, went for a drink with his buddies after work. At about 12:30 a.m., an individual he had charged with impaired driving in 1996 walked up and shot him in the back of the head, killing him instantly. Tom was married with three children.

In the days after the killing, I assisted the force psychologist in the Midland area, conducting a number of debriefings for police, paramedics, hospital personnel and the families of the Midland OPP members. It was a difficult time for everyone, but especially for Tom's family. The shooter was given a life sentence, with an opportunity for parole in 2022.

During the time I worked as an addiction counsellor, I assisted many officers experiencing alcohol- or drug-related problems. In some instances, the officers entered treatment programs such as the Donwood Institute in Toronto. But others weren't motivated and continued to drink. To a large extent, alcohol was the drug of choice for the officers.

The OPP Command Staff were very supportive of the program and there was never any reluctance on their part to support officers who sought help. One of my proudest moments occurred when I received a letter of commendation from Comm. Tom O'Grady for assisting an officer who had alcohol-related issues. It stated in part: "I acknowledge, appreciate and commend you for your success in dealing with the most private and difficult personal crises faced by our members and their families."

I didn't think about Larry Talbot during the first few years in my new role but in November 1997, I read a newspaper article about Steven Truscott, who had agreed to undergo DNA testing to prove he did not kill Lynne Harper. This was exciting news, because Truscott wasn't in a position to know if there was any forensic material remaining from the 1959 homicide, and if he did kill Lynne, he was leaving himself wide open. But if he was innocent, this would be a conclusive method to prove it.

It struck me as an opportune time to once again contact the OPP with a request that they investigate Larry Talbot, and this time to include the Lynne Harper homicide in the report. I wasn't certain how this addition would be accepted, but knew this additional hypothesis was essentially suggesting that the iconic Comm.

Harold Graham arrested the wrong person for the murder. I also wondered if it might affect an investigation of Talbot in the other cases. I completed the report in the latter part of December 1997. It included the opening premise:

The following report considers the probability that Larry Talbot is responsible for the murder of Pauline Ivy Dudley on August 21, 1973 and should also be considered a suspect in the murder of Lynne Harper, June 9, 1959, as well as a number of other unsolved homicides of women in Ontario.[1]

The report contained much of the information I've included in the book:

- The cottage invasion on June 29, 1971.
- The Pauline Ivy Dudley homicide.
- Larry Talbot's employment history.
- Talbot arrested on Second Avenue North at Sauble Beach, peeking in a bedroom window.
- Some references from the first report, requesting surveillance (Project Tree) including: Christine Prince, Delia Adriano, Les Church, Det. Sgt. Barry Browning, audio tapes of conversations with Les Church and Bill Elliott.
- Christine Prince, Delia Adriano, Valerie Stevens, Cindy Halliday, Jenny Isford, Linda Shaw all included in the *Toronto Star* article.
- Project Tree — March 31, 1983, surveillance team's observations May 6, 1983.
- Talbot stopped for speeding and discovered he was on the police computer.
- Possible psychological issues.
- Court transcript — Judge Mossop's pre-sentence comments in the case of our cottage invasion.
- Talbot's lack of remorse, based on his comments when I escorted him to the Walkerton County Jail.
- The Lynne Harper homicide, including the reasons I believed he should be considered a person of interest.

The following is the verbatim portion of the report specifically related to the Harper case:

a. **Talbot's Vehicle** — Talbot was driving a 1957 Chevrolet Bel Air 2 door-210- Baby Blue, with a cream top and cream inside the chrome fins. According to Bill Elliott*, he drove this vehicle from 1957 to 1960.

The 1957 Chevrolet similar to the one driven by Talbot in June 1959.

At Steven Truscott's trial, which commenced September 16, 1959 in Goderich, OPP Constable Tremblay (sic) testified that the following were Truscott's exact words regarding the car that stopped for Lynne Harper. "It was a 1959 Chev. Bel Air model grey, with a lot of chrome on it and white-walled tires." He also declared that Steven had said the car had yellow markers. . . . The boy's mother said he told her of "a late-model Chevrolet."[2]

(Note to readers: Trumbley was actually the second officer to speak to Steven. The first was Const. Donald Hobbs, who spoke to him June 10. At trial Hobbs testified: "I asked him if he saw Lynne again and he said he did look back and saw her getting into a car at the highway. He said it appeared to be a late-model Chevrolet and that there was a lot of chrome on the car. It could be a Bel Air version and that it appeared to have a yellow licence plate.[3] The information regarding Hobbs wasn't included in the report.)

I believe that it could have been a Chevrolet Truscott observed, but a 1957 model, not a 1959. Truscott, in his initial encounter with Trumbley, apparently stated that he "thought" it was a 1959 "with a lot of chrome." The 1957 Chevrolet has a lot of chrome, and the 1959 does not. Truscott also described the vehicle as being "grey." On the evening in question, LeBourdais' book included the fact that "it was still bright daylight. The sun would not set for more than an hour."[4]

If the sun was reflecting on the Chevrolet in question and a person was standing approximately 1,300 feet from the vehicle, what colour would that person see? I asked two of my artist friends this question. The one friend advised me that because of the distance and light colour of the vehicle (turquoise), it would be seen as a grey colour and the darker the colour of a vehicle, the darker the colour observed by the witness. My other friend suggested that the effect of the sun reflecting on the turquoise colour would result in a grey image. (I haven't found any reference in the LeBourdais book to indicate that this issue was addressed by either the prosecution or defense teams.)

(Note to readers: The chrome on the 1957 Chevrolet- Model 210 driven by Talbot included a chrome strip the length of the vehicle, which becomes a chrome spear on the rear fenders, chrome on the tips of the rear fenders, chromed rear bumper with chrome bumperettes, chrome front bumper, including grill, chrome metal V ornament on trunk lid, chrome metal V on the hood, chrome around the headlights, two chrome arrows on the hood and a chrome strip the length of the front and back windows. The 1959 Chevrolet Bel Air has a narrow chrome strip the length of the vehicle, chrome on the front bumper, but not as wide as the 1957, and chrome on the rear bumper, but 10 centimetres narrower than the '57, a recessed chrome front grill and small chrome spears on the front of both front fenders and chrome around the rear tail lights.)

A 1959 Chevrolet Steven thought Lynne entered.

b. **Blood:** During the trial, evidence was presented that blood was found at the crime scene both on the deceased as well as around her. The blood was described as Group A and under cross-examination Mr. Donnelly received admittance from both Dr. Penistan and the laboratory technician Elgin Brown that about 42 per cent of the population has Group A blood."[5]

There are two separate occasions when Talbot's blood type was obtained:

On July 2, 1971, Talbot was a suspect in the homicide of two women (May 6, 1970 – Moorby and May 19, 1970 – Ferguson — Palgrave area.) He submitted a sample of his saliva to Corporal Murray Peer, District Six Identification Unit, Mount Forest. It tested as Group A.

On October 18, 1982, I was advised by Detective Inspector Donaldson that Talbot's blood had been submitted to the Centre of Forensic Sciences for grouping purposes was tested as Group A — Secretor status — CFS file#3968-80 — reference Micheline St. Amour homicide.

(Note to reader: Talbot's 1971 identification photo bore an uncanny resemblance to the composite of the person wanted in the slayings of Doreen Moorby, shot at her Gormley home on May 6, 1970 , and Margaret Ferguson, shot to death on May 19, 1970 at her Palgrave residence, about 40 kilometres north of the Pearson International Airport on Highway 50. An extensive investigation was conducted by the OPP CIB in 1971. He was eventually ruled out, and 29 years later, 52-year-old Ronald West, an ex Toronto cop, was charged and convicted of the homicides and sentenced to life imprisonment. Talbot had also been investigated in connection with the 1980 murder of Micheline St. Amour in the North Bay area, but was eliminated as a suspect. It remains a cold case.)

c. **Shoe Imprints:** In LeBourdais' book, the following passage relates to the possibility that the killer left two indentations in the ground a "few inches below or west of the girl's feet."

Two very conspicuous pushed-back earth marks were described by some of those present that afternoon as being a few inches below or west of the girl's feet each ten to eleven inches long and in their opinion caused by the full length of the inside edges of a pair of shoes worn by someone in a prone position with his feet turned sideways. It was taken for granted by airmen, police and doctors that these marks were made by the feet of the attacker."[6]

The forest floor that witnessed the violent death of Lynne

On October 11, 1978, Talbot was arrested after a woman saw him peering at her at a cottage at Sauble Beach. This was basically the same MO he had used on us in 1971, but on this occasion the hockey laces were replaced with tape and the cleaning rag mask was replaced with two silk stockings. He also painted the running shoes black. The running shoes in question were a size 9, and from the measuring instrument included in the photograph, they measure 11 inches in length. I have the original photographs and will release them [to an investigator] when contacted for same.[7]

d. **Body Comparisons:** Dr. Penistan at the preliminary hearing testified the "marks by the girl's feet were made by the attacker in a prone position..." according to LeBourdais.

And Dr. Brooks was more "graphic" testifying "how the murderer's feet had been turned out sideways, with toes slightly upwards towards the body, and the full length of the inner edges of the soles pushing against the earth..."[8] This activity caused furrows which were "about six inches below or west of the girl's feet."[9]

Lynne Harper was 5'3" and with this additional 6" (while not exact) was close to Larry Talbot's height of 5'10".

(Note to reader: This wasn't in the report sent to the OPP.)

e. **The Reef Knot:** In LeBourdais' book there is reference to the killer securing a reef knot around Harper's neck under her left jaw using part of Harper's sleeveless blouse.[10] Not everyone is adept at tying this knot. My guess is that boaters and Boy Scouts would be two groups that saw a need for same and Talbot was a member of the Boy Scouts according to his personnel file at Industrial Plumbing.

f. **Crime Scene Neatness:** In both the Halliday and Dudley homicides, the victim's shoes were placed next to the body. (And in terms of the Harper crime scene, Lynne's "turquoise shorts lay right next to her elbow, her shoes about a foot away."[11]) In the Harper homicide, the deceased clothes were all "very orderly put down." In the Halliday homicide, the victim's coat was "left neatly folded" near a road. I am not aware of the crime scenes relative to Adriano, Stevens, Shaw, and Halliday, but I refer you to the remarks by LeBourdais regarding the Crime Scene Orderliness in the Harper killing (Page 9 of this report) for comparison purposes, regarding these victims as well as other unsolved homicides in the province.

Page 9 of the report included the following :

Crime Scene Orderliness

The outstanding feature of the scene in Lawson's Bush was its orderliness. This was not a man who tossed his victim into a ditch by the road, or even hid her body in some swamp or thicket miles away, where it might not be found for weeks or months. … He laid her neatly in one of many hollows and went back for her clothes (dropping panties partway into the bush) either in the car, or some place near-by where the attack had taken place.

… He zippered up her turquoise shorts, turned them
right side out, and placed the shorts, shoes, socks
and hair band so that they were "very orderly put
down," as Dr.(David) Brooks testified.

… He carefully twisted off the tough hardwood
saplings and laid them across the body as though
performing a ritual.[12]

(Note to reader: When I was reviewing the Dudley file after I
gave this report to the OPP, I discovered Pauline Dudley's body was
also covered with "grass and pine branches" but not to the extent
the farmer working in his field couldn't spot the body.)

I included several recommendations in the report for investigating Talbot:

Larry Talbot has travelled throughout Ontario since 1952 when
he began his employment with Industrial Plumbing.* Some examples of his extensive travel are cited in my previous report on him. In
reviewing his previous criminal activity, it's quite apparent that he
has violent tendencies. In the matter of Pauline Ivy Dudley, there is
a high probability that he was the perpetrator and if the investigators had the scientific technology that we have today, he probably
would have been indicted. In terms of Lynne Harper and what we
know about Talbot, including: opportunity, similar MO — Dudley
killing (grass on Dudley; branches on Harper) crime scene neatness,
personal characteristics, same make vehicle — it is imperative that
he be considered a suspect and investigated. He also can be connected in somewhat loose ways with other killings in the province
that I referred to in my previous report and ironically the *Toronto
Star* reporters also compiled their own analysis around 6 victims. The
reporters in this story originally focused on 130 unsolved murders
and then further examined the six that were subject of their featured article. I included both Adriano and Prince in my 1983 report
as well as Isford. I know very little about the Lynda Shaw killing so
won't comment further on this investigation. I also make mention
of the Cindy Halliday killing because of the placement of the shoes
that may be similar to Dudley and this taunting of investigators

by the perpetrator if the Harper killing and the Halliday killing were at the hands of the same suspect. Ironically Talbot received a speeding ticket on County Road 22 albeit a considerable time after the killing. But do killers return to the scene? He is also residing in Bracebridge.

I also included the comments from two of the investigators involved in the Adriano and Stevens cases — Halton Regional police Inspector John Van der Lelie and OPP Detective Inspector Rick Kotwa — who thought the similarities to other cases might be worth exploring:

Valerie Stevens was taken from Toronto to the Burford area near Brantford and two other victims have been left in a reasonable proximity to her body. They include Lynda White, who went missing November 14, 1968 from London and her body was discovered in the St. Williams area, May 9, 1973 and Jacqueline English, abducted from Wellington Road, London, on October 4, 1969 and found in a river in the Otterville area. (Note to readers: White's wallet was discovered at an excavation site in Burlington on May 9, 1973 and Talbot and White both lived in Burlington.) Christine Prince was abducted and taken a long distance to her death and also left in a river in the Scarborough area, which was approximately 7 minutes from Talbot's residence! Adriano was abducted from her property and found slain in the same general vicinity where Dudley was discovered.

I believe Talbot is aware of various lovers' lanes, isolated areas and other out-of-the-way places because of the travelling he's completed over the years with the various companies. There is the one instance where surveillance observed him in a lovers' lane area (Project Tree), but he's also had this penchant to prowl as noted in his previous criminal offenses at Sauble Beach. This pattern probably began sometime around the period he was caught looking in a window at Sauble Beach as a young man. He was also observed by myself and Prov. Const Paul Farroll (retired, Caledon Detachment) in the early a.m. walking through a back alley behind cottages at Sauble Beach. He fled when he spotted the cruiser, and we found a mop handle that he had been carrying in some bushes. (He was probably using the mop handle to reach into cottages through open windows to steal purses — as we did have theft complaints of this nature during that year and Talbot was a suspect.)

It is my opinion that Talbot should be the subject of a comprehensive investigation that considers the following homicides:

Pauline Ivy Dudley

Lynne Harper

Christine Prince

Delia Adriano

Jacqueline English

Lynda White

Valerie Stevens

Neda Novak

Constance Dickey

Cindy Halliday

(Note to reader: The Halton Regional Police included Neda Novak and Constance Dickey when they questioned Talbot, but were unable to tie him into either homicide. Henry Williams later confessed to these two killings.)

The investigation should also include those other homicides from the "cold files" that have sufficient similarities to the above homicides to also merit consideration for analysis.

Note: In terms of the Stevens, English, and White homicides, Les Church,* during our interview on February 3, 1983, circled both Simcoe and Woodstock as locations which had Industrial Plumbing customers.

These areas would be well known to Talbot in his sales role with this company. (See Appendix J- original map.)

(Note to reader: I read *On The Farm* by Stevie Cameron when I was writing this book. This was an insightful expose of the inept, apathetic response of the Vancouver Police Department during a period when women involved in the sex trade were murdered by Robert Pickton. There was a section of the book that caught my attention regarding Kim Rossmo, the first "working policeman" in Canada to receive a doctorate in criminology, specializing in "geographical profiling." An appraisal of Rossmo's work was published in the *Daily Telegraph* on April 22, 1999:

> By analyzing the locations of a series of crimes, the inventor of geographic profiling, Kim Rossmo, can find out a lot about a killer, because the geographic behaviour of humans is easy to understand. The offence might be pathological, but the locations of the crime sites are non pathological, he says. The same patterns that determine how we shop and where McDonalds will put its next restaurant apply to criminal [patterns]. People tend to go about their routine business close to where they live, work or play, giving all of us an activity space which is closely connected to our homes. Needing to bury a body, the places likely to occur to a murderer will fall within the area he is familiar with.[13]

How did Rossmo's theoretical construct equate with the cold cases in my report?

- Pauline Ivy Dudley: Crime scene to Talbot's residence – 15 minutes.
- Christine Prince: Crime scene to Talbots's residence – 7 minutes.
- Delia Adriano: 26 minutes to Talbot's residence.
- Lynne Harper: Industrial Plumbing customers in Goderich Clinton, Kincardine, Mitchell.
- Cindy Halliday: One hour from the crime scene to his residence.
- Jacqueline English and Lynda White: Talbot had customers in the London area.
- Sauble Beach crimes: Talbot's cottage in area where crimes occurred.
- Valerie Stevens: Crime scene at Burford to Talbot's residence – One hour 41 minutes.

- Lynda White: Crime scene at St.Williams to Talbot's residence – One hour and 31 minutes.

(At the time of the Adriano homicide, Talbot was residing in Scarborough. The 26-minute time frame for Adriano was the distance to his previous address in Burlington.)

I concluded the report with the following comments and recommendations:

It's my opinion that the allegations contained in this report will require those kinds of activities as recommended by Mr. Justice Archie G. Campbell for the investigation of an alleged "inter-jurisdictional serial killer." The following are some suggestions to consider:

1. Establish a task force including: Halton Regional Police, Metro Toronto Police Service, Ontario Provincial Police and the R.C.M.P.

I have included the R.C.M.P. for the following reasons:

- Lead Lynne Harper homicide — to alleviate any perception of bias in terms of the 1959 OPP investigation into the killing.
- Co-ordinate efforts for archival retrieval of registration logs that may exist from the Clinton Air Force Base.
- Liaison with New York State, Edmonton and Calgary authorities to establish the presence of any outstanding homicides — in particular young women hitchhikers. (Talbot travelled to these areas for either pleasure trips or on business.)
- Share in resources for project (personal (sic) and financial.)

2. Review the Pauline Ivy Dudley homicide including the hair exhibits for DNA examination. Consult with the Regional Crown Attorney regarding an indictment in this matter.
3. Complete a crime scene analysis and comparison of the: Harper, Dudley and Halliday crime scenes.
4. Review the "cold files' of outstanding homicides in Ontario — specifically of young women hitch-hikers or victims that were abducted.
5. Re-examine the Lynne Harper homicide with the purpose of including or eliminating him as a suspect.

6. Compare DNA material that's obtainable or on file from subject Talbot with any victim's DNA that's available.

7. Commence surveillance on Talbot between April and September 1998. If it's apparent that he's actively stalking potential victims, deploy a decoy policewoman to play the role of hitch-hiker. She should possess physical characteristics similar to Pauline Dudley.

8. If there is no activity regarding No.7, approach Talbot to take another polygraph examination regarding the Dudley homicide. When you consider his conversation with the previous polygraph operator (challenging etc.,) he may co-operate. If he does co-operate, the questioning should be focused on Dudley but also include a cluster of questions around the Harper homicide.

9. The Ministry of the Attorney General should be consulted following a re-examination of the Harper homicide. This consultation will be necessary to determine what information needs to be shared with Steven Truscott. If it is the opinion of the investigators that Larry Talbot is considered a suspect in this homicide, but there is insufficient evidence to indict him, then what is the Crown's responsibility in terms of disclosure to Truscott?

Conclusion

Larry Talbot has travelled extensively in Ontario since 1952 with a number of companies, including Industrial Plumbing. Talbot's role as a travelling salesman equipped with the ordinary automobiles, business suits and personable mannerisms would allay any anxieties or fears of a potential victim either about to enter his vehicle while hitch-hiking or answering a knock at the door. His job was essentially his alibi! (For example, he wasn't adverse (sic) to travelling long distances in short amounts of time. To what extent has this job-related necessity to travel, quickly removed him from crime scenes or given him the advantage of select/stalking his victims at random, as he travelled from customer to customer throughout the province? A serial killer couldn't elect a better occupation than that of the travelling salesman!)

We know he was investigated for the Dudley homicide, but if an alert patrol officer hadn't recorded his licence plate, would he still be categorized as the voyeuristic cottager preying on tourists at Sauble Beach? The Dudley homicide places Talbot in a different league. Does an individual with his psycho-social characteristics have the potential to continue to kill? Does Talbot have the potential to be violent? Have there been other victims? Is the Dudley homicide similar to the Harper killing? Is the English abduction and homicide similar to the Prince abduction and homicide? Is it a coincidence that Dudley and Adriano (who worked a mile from Talbot) were discovered in the same geographical area? Is it also a coincidence that English, White and Stevens were discovered in a reasonably close proximity in southwestern Ontario — and in reasonable proximity to two customers served by Industrial Plumbing in Woodstock and Simcoe?

These and many other questions can only be answered if there is an aggressive, co-ordinated, co-operative and adequately funded project. In my opinion, Larry Talbot deserves the kind of attention Mr. Justice Campbell recommended in his report to the Solicitor General and for all the same reasons! Please contact me for any further information or assistance.

Signed
J. Barry Ruhl, BA, B.S.W.,
Associate Counsellor Human Resources Branch, GHQ,
O.P.P. (Ret.)

The references to Mr. Justice Archie Campbell involve one of Canada's most famous murderers, Paul Bernardo, who was convicted of murdering Leslie Mahaffy in 1991 and Kristen French in 1992 and was the prime suspect in a large number of rapes that occurred in the Scarborough area. In 1996, Justice Campbell completed a review of the investigation of Bernardo, and his summary of recommendations included the following:

A major case management system is required for major and inter-jurisdictional serial predator investigations, based on:

- co-operation rather than rivalry (between police services)
- early recognition of linked offences[14]

When the report was finished I wasn't sure where to send it, until I learned a joint OPP-London police task force was reviewing 20 homicide cases of young women dating from 1956 that occurred in the London area. It was called Project Angel. I also knew the officer supervising the project, Insp. Mike Coughlin. We were members of the Six District Criminal Investigation Squad in 1976. This seemed a good fit, because Talbot had a number of customers in the London area, when he worked for Industrial Plumbing. I was particularly interested in the Jacqueline English homicide. Jacqueline was 15 years old when she disappeared, and was last seen on the evening of October 4, 1969, after leaving the Treasure Island Shopping Centre in the Highway 401-Wellington Road area of London. She was walking north on Wellington Road.

Her body was found in Big Otter Creek on October 6, 1969. She had been sexually assaulted and killed by a blow to the head. Big Otter Creek is about 13 kilometres east of Tillsonburg, about three kilometres west of the village of Otterville, 65 kilometres from where she was last seen walking on Wellington Road in London. Talbot had customers in both Tillsonburg and Woodstock, which are close to where English's body was discovered.

This homicide was somewhat similar to the Christine Prince murder: both victims were abducted while walking alone after dark, both were transported long distances, both were sexually assaulted and both victims suffered blows to the head and were left in creeks adjacent to wooded areas.

I met Mike Coughlin at Barrie OPP on March 28, 1998, and reviewed the report with him. He was going to give copies to both the co-ordinator at Project Angel and a unit reviewing the Steven Truscott investigation. I also included a memorandum for him that contained a number of recommendations:[15]

- Speak to Chief Supt. Wayne Frechette regarding this suspect. Wayne is reasonably in the know concerning him and may offer some suggestions around my recommendations and/or strategies to consider in addressing this subject.
- Contact the officers involved in collecting the historical data on the Steven Truscott/Lynne Harper occurrence, specifically in terms of crime scene exhibits for comparison with my suspect.
- Refer to the enclosed March 1983 report and tape regarding the suspect's business connections, job related stressors and description of him and vehicle ref. Jacqueline English.
- Determine if CISO (Criminal Intelligence Service Ontario) should play a role in this, regarding the multi-police jurisdictions.
- Contact CFS (Centre of Forensic Sciences) regarding any samples they may have regarding the St. Armour homicide in North Bay.
- Have your investigators contact me for some other material which will be of interest to you in this investigation (handwriting samples, photos of suspect and original footprints from the Sauble Beach occurrence.)
- If the subject of this report is eliminated as a suspect in the cases I have discussed, including the Steven Truscott matter, I want to know, as I also need closure.

I ended the memorandum with the following:

> Mike, as I mentioned in my most recent report, it will require a concerted effort of all concerned to either indict or eliminate this subject. The other reality is that he is not getting any younger. In my opinion, he's probably Ontario's Ted Bundy! He is not stupid and for a number of reasons has escaped detection, as I mention in the report.
>
> My thoughts are with you and please call me at any time for clarifications etc.

I do request a call from you in approximately a month's time. I don't need to know the operational strategies but simply a follow up call regarding the report status.

All the best,
J. Barry Ruhl, (Ret. OPP)

On November 5, 1998, I received a letter from Coughlin.[16]

Dear Barry:

I am returning your original materials concerning Talbot. We have retained a copy for our files. As indicated to you previously the information concerning Talbot has also been forwarded to the Harper investigators. You will be advised if any further information concerning Talbot comes to our attention.

Thank you for your concern.

Sincerely,
Mike Coughlin, Detective Inspector

Prior to receiving the letter from Coughlin, I contacted Project Angel on October 6, because I hadn't heard from anyone at the project. I spoke to Bill Smith, who thought he remembered me from a drug investigation, Project Scam, in the Bracebridge area. He told me that as a result of my recommendations to Coughlin, there was a cold squad being set up by the Criminal Investigation Bureau. He also sent my report to Det. Sgt. Pauline Schwantz in Mount Forest, who was working on the Truscott file and didn't think there was any DNA remaining from the Harper homicide.

Then, he told me something very interesting. The analyst assigned to Project Angel and Smith knew Ron Allan, the analyst assigned to Project Tree in 1983. According to Smith, Allan didn't think Talbot was involved in *any* of the homicides included in my report.

In fairness to Allan, the training and technology used in 1999 were more advanced than in 1983, when Allan was an analyst on Project Tree. But it made me wonder if Allan had been responsible for advising the brass that information in my report was false?

CHAPTER 7

A PERSON OF DISINTEREST

On October 14, 1998, I called Pauline Schwantz. She was assisting Det. Insp. Jim Wilson of the CIB in investigating persons of interest reported to the police by the public in the Truscott case.

On July 6, 2000, Heather Bird had written an article in the *Toronto Sun* about the ongoing investigation. "Det. Insp. Jim Wilson . . . has been working on the case since 1997 . . . and the OPP have now identified and are actively investigating 12 to14 'persons of interest,' Wilson said, 'It's very difficult to commence an investigation into various people's backgrounds and whereabouts 40 years ago. You don't know where it leads."[1]

Schwantz told me she had read my report and forwarded it to Wilson. She said the OPP did an "excellent job" investigating the Harper homicide and believed Truscott was guilty. She said she was meeting with Wilson the following week and would contact me after the meeting.

In the notes I made following our conversation, I wrote: "It sounds like Pauline is convinced Truscott was the culprit and believes I would feel the same way if I had access to the trial's transcripts"[2] I never heard from Schwantz and when I called her November 2, she said Wilson was going to read the report in November and was working on another tip with "lots more to it." She suggested I call him. I left a message for Wilson, who was away until November 23, inquiring about the status of my report.

On November 30 he called. He had just returned from New Brunswick and hadn't read the report. I asked him how much time he needed and he replied two months, because he was busy with 20 cases. I asked him if he had shared the report with anyone and he said he hadn't, and after he read it, he'd decide what he'd do. He suggested I call him in a couple of months. He also said he remembered Larry Talbot and my interest in him during the 1980s. (Wilson was a member of the Seven District Crime Squad I supervised and was aware of my belief that Talbot may be a serial killer.) I jokingly said, "I suppose you're thinking, 'Oh there goes Ruhl again!'" and he laughed. He also repeated the fact he hadn't shared the report with either his immediate supervisor, Det. Supt. Larry Edgar, director of the CIB, or Chief Supt. Wayne Frechette, Edgar's boss.

I was concerned about Wilson's response to my report. I wrote in my journal: "The fact that he has had a report this long and hadn't taken time to read it doesn't hold much promise of any action by him. It's interesting that he'll take the time to travel to New Brunswick to interview witnesses regarding the Truscott matter, but not take time to read a report which at the slowest speed could be read and somewhat digested in an hour or so."[3]

Because of my concerns, I contacted Wilson's supervisor, Det. Supt. Larry Edgar. Larry and I worked at Kitchener and were on the same platoon in the early 1970s. He was an excellent investigator and very effective at catching the bad guys. (Larry was the first officer to arrest the prolific Mitchell "Mickey" McArthur. McArthur was a career criminal who amassed nearly 200 criminal convictions and during a bank robbery in Port Perry, Ont., in 1994, he shot and wounded three policemen. He's currently serving a lengthy prison sentence.)

After Larry was promoted to corporal, he became a member of the OPP Outlaw Biker Squad responsible for gathering intelligence on the biker gangs in Ontario. He was later promoted to inspector and investigated a number of homicides, as a member of the CIB. In 1997, he was promoted to director of the CIB.

On December 4, 1998, I met Edgar at Barrie, reviewed the report with him and discussed my concern regarding Wilson's apparent lack of interest. I recall Larry saying "I wonder what 'HH' would think of this!" a reference used by many OPP personnel when they spoke about former OPP Comm. Harold Hopkins Graham, and said he'd give Chief Supt. Wayne Frechette and the Behavioural Sciences Unit copies of the report for inclusion in the ViCLAS program. I suggested sending a copy of the report to Comm. Gwen Boniface, OPP commissioner from 1998 to 2006, but he said she'd just return it to him. He said he'd call me in a couple of weeks, because he was presently in the middle of a trial.

The ViCLAS (Violent Crime Linkage Analysis System) is designed to collect information about the victim, offender/suspect description, modus operandi, forensic and behavioural data. The [ViCLAS] questionnaires are processed at the Provincial ViCLAS Centre at OPP Headquarters in Orillia. The program was explained in the *OPP Review Winter 2007/08*:

> Since January 2007, ViCLAS has potentially linked
> 152 Ontario cases through behavioral analysis.
> In relation to those cases, 23 were confirmed
> links involving sexual assaults and one case was
> a confirmed link to a homicide. ViCLAS identi-
> fied the unknown offender in each of these cases
> based upon the verbal, physical and sexual behavior
> exhibited by the offenders in previous known
> offender submissions.[4]

Larry didn't contact me, so I called him on January 15, 1999. He said Jim Wilson was busy working on a missing person investigation in New Liskeard and told me to call him in the future instead of Wilson. He also said he'd read "half" of the report and there were things that needed to be "looked at." He had given a copy of the report to Chief Supt. Wayne Frechette, but didn't know if he'd read it.

On February 5, I called Edgar a few days after the *Toronto Star* had run a story on ViCLAS under the headline "OPP to reopen 150 unsolved murder cases."[5] I asked him if Pauline Dudley would be included and he replied in the affirmative. I also asked if Wilson was working on the Talbot file, but he said he was still in New Liskeard. He suggested I call him the following Monday, because the investigators call and discuss their cases with him.

I later wondered why Edgar simply didn't call or e-mail Wilson to inquire about the status of the report.

On February 9, I called Edgar and he still hadn't contacted Wilson, but told me he would page him and get back to me. I never received a call.

On February 16, Wilson called my home while I was in Toronto. My wife told him I would be home the following day, but Wilson said he was going away on business for a week or a week and a half. I left a message for him anyway on February 18, but didn't get a response.

On March 2, a letter was faxed to Comm. Gwen Boniface and Deputy Comm. Moe Pilon by my lawyer, because it was evident nothing was being done with the report. We thought by moving our concern up the chain of command to the Commissioner, it might get things rolling. It included the following:

> Barry's concerns admit of two possibilities, of
> course. A criminal investigation may support Barry's
> concern. On the other hand, a criminal investigation
> could conclude that Barry's concerns are mistaken.
> Even if Barry is ultimately mistaken, however, it
> would seem prudent in the circumstances to make
> sure he is.[6]

The same day the letter was sent, I received a voice message from Chief Supt. Wayne Frechette:

> Hi, this is a message for Barry. It's Wayne Frechette,
> and it's March 2, about 4:20. You sent some mate-
> rial into Larry Edgar's shop into CIB some time
> ago, and I'm groping for exactly how long ago, but

in any event they sent me over a copy and I think
it's been a case of Larry thought I had gotten back
to you to acknowledge it, and I assumed he had.
As a result neither one of us did. So here I am on
bended knee, somewhat. What I've done with the
file is sent it over to Behavioural Sciences for them
to put it through the mill in terms of linkage and
similarities and this and that and the other, and
when they get it back to me I'll decide next what to
do with it. If you need to talk phone anytime ... but
I thought I would acknowledge, yeah, we did have it,
and we didn't toss it out, and it's being looked at as
we speak. Thanks. Bye bye.

The voicemail was troubling. It appeared Frechette and Edgar
had never met to discuss the report, because Frechette didn't know
Larry and I had spoken on a number of occasions following our
meeting December 4. It also made me wonder if Edgar had sent
the report to the BSU, as he had said he would, since Frechette
indicated he would do that.

Frechette was a smart cop. I met him when I supervised the
Seven District Crime Squad and had invited him to be guest
speaker at a squad meeting, where he discussed the role and strategies he used when he was a polygraph operator. He'd obtained a
BA in Psychology when most cops in the OPP, like me, had just
enough education to be accepted. Like Harold Graham, Bill
Lidstone, Larry Edgar, and Jim Wilson, he also had been a member
of the CIB, eventually attaining the rank of chief superintendent.

Frechette knew more about Talbot than most officers in the organization. He was a member of the Project Tree surveillance team
and we had a number of discussions during the project. He also had
been involved in the Cindy Halliday homicide investigation.

Several months passed following his call to me and I didn't hear
from the OPP. But, on July 8, I received a voice mail from Det. Staff
Sgt. Mary McLaughlin of the CIB.

Barry, its Mary McLaughlin from *CIB Major Cases* ... Just to
let you know, I'm reviewing the file that was forwarded to Wayne

Frechette and subsequently went to Behavioural Sciences Unit. To let you know I'm following up on this … Maybe we can touch base next week sometime when you're around and we can discuss the file. I'd be really interested to talk to you.

On July 19, I received another call from Mary, with whom I had worked in the Peer Support Program. She reiterated that she was assigned to follow up on the Talbot investigation. She was a member of the Unsolved Homicide Unit and believed Durham and Halton Regional police, as well as Project Angel, were interested in Talbot, but she didn't know if it was going to be a joint project. She said Sgt. Steve Smethurst, an analyst in the BSU, told her Talbot could be linked to three homicides with the potential for others. She also told me Smethurst wanted any information I had on Talbot for inclusion in the ViCLAS program. We were scheduled to meet July 27 but she cancelled the meeting.

I didn't hear from Mary again, but when I reached her, she said she'd contacted the Coroner's Office (at the Centre of Forensic Sciences, in Toronto) to determine if Halton Regional had re-sent the Dudley exhibits to the centre. She had initiated this follow up because there was a new method of testing for DNA called "mito-chondrial analysis." The process involved comparing the hair found in Talbot's vehicle with Dudley's mother's to determine if there was a genetic match.

She said she had discussed the Dudley homicide with Larry Edgar and they both questioned the fact Talbot wasn't indicted for the murder. I asked about Durham Regional's involvement and if it concerned the Christine Jessup case.

Jessup was a nine-year-old who had been abducted from the side of her home in Queensville on October 3, 1984. Her battered remains were found on December 31, 1984 on Concession 4 near the village of Sunderland on Highway 12, about 40 kilometres from Sunderland in Durham Region.

Mary said she thought it was the Debbie Silverman case. Silverman, 21, was kidnapped August 12, 1978, at about 5 a.m. from the foyer of her apartment building in downtown Toronto. She was taken to a lovers' lane and murdered, and her body was discovered

November 12, 1978 in a shallow grave, just one concession south of where Jessup's body was found a few years later.

Talbot's cottage was an hour north of these crime scenes.

I included in my journal notes: "Mary sounded very enthusiastic about getting involved in the investigation, and before ending our conversation stated it would be 'us' doing it!"[7]

It might or it might not be important, but was and am aware that my wife Pat, Dudley, and Silverman all had similar facial and hair characteristics.

Facial and hair similarities of Pat Ruhl, Pauline
Dudley and Debbie Silverman.

On September 1, 1999, Mary and I met for three and a half hours
at my residence. I walked her through my journey with Talbot and
during the meeting, she said she received a memo from Frechette,
assigning her to the investigation and instructing her to contact Sgt.
Steve Smethurst of the Behavioural Sciences Unit. But, she wasn't
given a copy of my report, which I thought was odd, and I gave
her a copy. (When she called on July 8, she said she was reviewing

"the file," and apparently my report wasn't included in the "file" she was reviewing.)

The salient points of what I thought was a very productive meeting were as follows:

- She was going to check with Jim Wilson and determine the DNA status of Truscott.
- She wanted to consider using me as a part-time constable in the investigation.
- She had no opinion regarding the Lynne Harper homicide because she needed to do some research, including the LeBourdais book and CIB files.
- She wanted to review the Project Tree file.
- She told me if Sgt. Smethurst was given enough information, he could initiate a linkage analysis in the Pauline Dudley and Lynne Harper homicides.
- She told me she wasn't in this for rewards or career enhancement but to right a wrong, "if it's there."
- I told Mary I saw her role as the coordinator of a project that was going to either include or eliminate Truscott.
- I also emphasized the fact James Lockyer was Truscott's lawyer and it was best that the OPP resolved this issue because Lockyer would be relentless in his pursuit.
- Mary said she'd update me on her progress.
- I gave her all the files I had and explained their significance and she noted each one.
- When we finished Mary said, "I'll do the best I can."

On September 22, I received a call from McLaughlin. She said she had contacted the Halton Regional Police and they were "non-committal" about releasing any information to her on the Dudley file, but requested any information that would assist them. She also said someone at the OPP headquarters called the Harper case "highly political."

On October 7, McLaughlin called after reviewing the files we discussed at our meeting. She was interested in the murder of a woman from Smith Falls who was stabbed to death, because Talbot was known to carry knives. She also recovered the file from OPP archives I sent to Det. Insp. Barry Thompson regarding the Cindy Halliday homicide. She didn't know if it had been assigned to anyone following Thompson's death.

Then, McLaughlin made a very disappointing revelation: She wouldn't be investigating the Truscott matter and hadn't seen any of the Truscott reports because Insp. Jim Wilson was assigned to the investigation. And she had decided not to contact Wilson regarding any DNA evidence.

She said she was following up on the other cold cases included in the report, but only during her spare time because of other duties and court appearances. I wrote the following in my journal notes:

> She has no opinion regarding the Truscott-Talbot
> hypothesis because my report is based on the
> LeBourdais book and newspaper reports and not on
> case files. And Steve Smethurst included in his BSU
> report the notion that my report is unsubstantiated
> because of the source of the information. He would
> need actual reports for analysis. She also suggested
> that Harper was neat and folded her own clothes
> before she was raped and murdered! But she also
> commented that the report has "food for thought,"
> including the fact Talbot had a similar vehicle.[8]

McLaughlin also said my involvement in the case was simply something she "threw out," and reviewed a report which cautioned that I shouldn't be involved as I was "too close to the investigation."[9] (McLaughlin's comment regarding my involvement in the case was simply something she "threw out" referred to her suggestion at the September 1 meeting, that I could be sworn in as a part time constable and play an active role in the investigation.) And I don't know the report she's referring to about me being "too close to the investigation." I think some folks reading the book, or the OPP who are named in this story, may wonder if I've made the facts of various cases fit because I had a grudge against Talbot. This is simply not the case. I've always been up-front about my personal interest in

Talbot and never made any effort to hide or downplay my personal interest in him.

I told her I wasn't happy with the way the file was being handled. I said the OPP had had the report for more than a year and were dragging their feet, which was incredible considering the implications. I told her General Headquarters was going to be contacted. I was very upset and wrote in my journal:

> Mary is much more tight-lipped from my previous
> conversations with her. It was my sense that she was
> going to do the Truscott matter along with the rest
> but it sounds like what I had originally suspected
> that she will be doing what she could between other
> assignments and Wilson will drag his feet on the
> Truscott matter-not good considering how much
> time has elapsed with little really done. Sounds like
> someone has spoken to her![10]

Following my October 7 conversation with McLaughlin, when she said she wasn't investigating the Truscott matter, I contacted my lawyer, who called general headquarters and expressed our disappointment.

On October 26 Mary called. She sounded angry and stated I made the call and she was disappointed because she had spoken to me a number of times.

I told her my concern wasn't with her specifically but with the OPP, who were dragging their feet on the Truscott matter. She said she had to write a report and include the conversations we had. She was going to ask to be removed from the investigation. She also said she contacted Halton Regional police regarding the "other women." I asked her if it included Delia Adriano, and she replied that it did and she was told Adriano was discovered 40 kilometres from the Dudley crime scene and not "in the same geographical area, as stated in my report." She said the suspect in the Adriano homicide (as described by witnesses) doesn't resemble Talbot. She was also embarrassed when she inquired about [Neda] Novak, only to discover someone was arrested for her homicide. I reminded her that an investigator's task is to either eliminate or include persons of interest during an investigation.

She said I was probably frustrated nobody was getting back to me regarding the investigation, but couldn't because I was retired (an interesting statement considering the investigative information she shared with me during our telephone conversations). I reminded her I simply wanted a courtesy call. She also informed me she couldn't be assigned to an investigation as the investigator because she didn't hold the rank of inspector. The conversation ended when she told me we were simply going in circles.[11]

That was my final conversation with the OPP. I took long walks after that, trying to make sense of the dynamics at play regarding my report and my relationship with the OPP. It seemed the file on Larry Talbot was going to be relegated to the archives and the historical facts supporting the iconic Harold Graham would remain intact.

However, that wasn't quite the case when Talbot was visited by the OPP at his residence 11 months after my final conversation with Mary McLaughlin.

On September 27, 2000, Det. Sgt. Pauline Schwantz interviewed Larry Talbot at his residence regarding the Lynne Harper homicide. The interview was conducted in the kitchen, with his wife present. It began at 12:25 p.m. and concluded at 1:04 p.m.:

Q: Do you recall where you worked in 1959?

A: I worked for the Industrial Plumbing Company* out of Toronto from 1951 to 1960. I was an industrial salesman selling plumbing supplies. When I went on the road in 1955 and at that time covered the Hamilton area. From then I did several areas including the Stratford-Kitchener area. I couldn't say where in particular I was at any time.

Q: Can you tell me if you ever went to the Clinton Air Force Base?

A: No. I never did.

Q: Did you know of the base?

A: Yes I had a relative there, Greg Germaine.*

Q: What do you know of the Lynn (sic) Harper homicide?

A: Just what I read in the paper. I heard that Truscott is trying to prove his innocence.

Q: Where did you live at the time?

A: On Livingstone Road,* which, no actually that's wrong. In 1958 we moved to Brantford* and bought a house on Inkerman Street,* where we lived 'til 1973. I lived there with my wife Sue* and we had 2 children.

Q: What type of car did you have in 1959?

A: A '57 Chevy. It was blue and white. The roof was white and it had a fin riding down the side of the car that was white. The body was robin's egg blue. It was a 210, a 2 door. I had the car from 1957 to 1960. That was a company car owned by Industrial Plumbing and I used it as personal also. We would go to Sauble Beach in it on the weekends.

Q: Would you be away doing sales overnight?

A: Yes. Mainly in London, Sarnia or Windsor in Southwestern Ontario.

Q: What type of car did you get in 1960?

A: A bronze 1960 Pontiac. I remember my cars.

Q: What type of licence plates would be on your 57 Chevy?

A: I think probably blue and white. I'm not colour conscious because I'm colour blind.

Q: Would you ever have yellow plates?

A: No, never. They had yellow in the 30's but not since I've been driving.

Q: Have you ever been on the Clinton base?

A: Only driven by it on Hwy 4. I never did any business in Clinton.

Q: Would you be willing to take a polygraph test regarding this incident?

A: Ya, I'd take it. I've got nothing to be afraid of or hide. When you say the name Lynn (sic) Harper I wouldn't have recognized it. I only knew the name Truscott.

Q: Did your wife have a car besides your company car?

A: In 1959 she had a white '56 Ford.*

Signed: Larry Talbot

P. Schwantz, D/Sgt. #7605[12]

The questioning by Schwantz was superficial and it would be interesting to know if her belief in Truscott's guilt was a mitigating factor in the report's brevity. But she did ask if he would take a polygraph and he responded in the affirmative. Why wasn't it done?

Q - What do you know of the Lynn Harper homicide?

A - Just what I read in the paper. I heard that Truscott is trying to prove his innocence.

Q - Where did you live at the time?

A - On ████████, no actually that's wrong. In 1958 we moved to ███████ and bought a house on ██████████ where we lived 'til 1973. I lived there with my wife ████████ ████████

Q - What type of car did you have in 1959?

A - A '57 Chevy. It was blue and white. The roof was white and it had a fin riding down the side of the car that was white. The body was a robin's egg blue. It was a 210, a 2 door. I had that car from 1957 to 1960. That was a company car owned by ███████ and I used it as personal also. We would go to Sauble Beach in it on the weekends.

Q - Would you be away doing sales overnight?

A - Yes. Mainly in London, Sarnia or Windsor in Southwestern Ontario.

Q - What type of car did you get in 1960?

A - A bronze 1960 Pontiac. I remember my cars.

Q - What type of licence plates would be on your 57 Chevy?

A - I think probably blue and white. I'm not colour conscious because I'm colour blind.

Q - Would you ever have yellow plates?

A - No, never. They had yellow in the 30's but not since I've been driving.

Q - Have you ever been on the Clinton base?

A - Only driven by it on Hwy 4. I never did any business in Clinton.

Q - Would you be willing to take a polygraph test regarding this incident?

A - Ya, I'd take it. I've got nothing to be afraid of or hide. When you say the name Lynn Harper I wouldn't have recognised it. I only knew the name Truscott.

Q - Did your wife have a car besides your company car?

A - In 1959 she had a black '55 Hillman, a small English car.

Signed: ████████
P. SCHWANTZ , D/Sgt. #7605

The interview report September 27, 2000 at Talbot's residence.

It's also difficult to understand why Schwantz did not pursue the issue when Talbot denied being on the air force base since the base was an Industrial Plumbing customer.

CHAPTER 8

THE KAUFMAN INQUIRY

On May 16, 2000, lawyers from the Association in Defence of the Wrongly Convicted (AIDWYC) announced they were applying for a "690" Review in the Steven Truscott case. Such a review can have three possible outcomes: refer the case to the Court of Appeal; a quashing of the conviction and order of a new trial; or dismissal of the application.

In *Until You Are Dead*, Sher said such reviews are usually based on new matters of significance, either not considered by the original court, or which arose after appeals. To be successful, "The applicant need not convince the minister of innocence or even prove conclusively a miscarriage had *actually* occurred." Rather, all that is needed is a demonstration that "a miscarriage of justice *likely* occurred."[1]

When I learned Truscott was applying for a review, I wanted to give his lawyers the information I had accumulated but I didn't know if I was in a legal position to be able to do so. On April 7, 2001, Pat and I went to Toronto to meet with Edward Greenspan of Greenspan, Heinein and White. He is one of the most prominent lawyers in the country and was involved in a television series called The *Scales of Justice*, which had featured a segment on the Lynne

Harper homicide. He wanted to review my report and provisions in the Criminal Code to see if I, as a former OPP officer, would be in "breach of trust" by providing information to Truscott's lawyers.

On May 28, Todd White an associate of Greenspan's, advised me he and Greenspan had read my report and believed there was a "strong circumstantial case" against Larry Talbot. He said they would contact James Lockyer, Truscott's lawyer, and without revealing my name, would tell him a retired OPP officer had information relevant to the Lynne Harper homicide.

On August 9, White spoke to Lockyer, who asked if Barry Ruhl was White's client. Lockyer said he received correspondence from the Ministry of the Attorney General, including a report and covering memorandum signed by me.[2] (The pages relating to the Pauline Ivy Dudley homicide were redacted.) He also had received a report from Steve Smethurst, an analyst with the OPP Behavioural Sciences Unit, and the Talbot "Interview Report" provided by Schwantz. Lockyer wanted to meet me, but White indicated he wanted to contact the Attorney General's office first to obtain permission.

On October 5, I received a call from Lockyer's partner, Phillip Campbell. He said there were five potential "suspects" referenced in the application for the 690 Review. This was based on the Truscott files the lawyers had received from the OPP, which the force was required by law to release.[3] Campbell said he didn't think much had been done in terms of investigating Talbot. He read a paragraph that referred to Talbot: "This subject was brought to our attention by a retired Det. Sgt. in the OPP. He drove a Chevrolet and travelled in the area."

But Campbell said because of the passage of time and lack of evidence, other potential suspects weren't as relevant as medical and witness evidence.

He asked why I was involved in the case, and I told him because I believed in the justice system. He said my report raised a "red flag" that could point to Talbot as a serial killer.

On October 9, White called me. He said he had spoken to Rose Carnaviera at the Attorney General's office, who suggested I speak to her or Det. Insp. Jim Wilson. She told White that in the copy of my report sent by the Attorney General to Lockyer, the section on Dudley was redacted because that was still an active investigation. White and Greenspan suggested I meet with Carnaviera.

The revelation that Lockyer had received a redacted report was upsetting since Dudley's death, probably at the hands of Larry Talbot, and the comparison between the Dudley and Harper homicides was the cornerstone of the report. After reading the unedited version of the report, Greenspan and White had concluded it made a "strong circumstantial case" against Talbot. But Lockyer was at a distinct disadvantage with the redacted version. I contacted his office and scheduled a meeting for December 13.

When we met, I reminded him I had to be careful with what I disclosed because of my previous occupation. Lockyer showed me the redacted pages and a copy of my journal notes, which were to a large extent illegible.[4]

I discussed the 30 months I had spent attempting to persuade the OPP to investigate Talbot and the abysmal results. I told him Greenspan and White read an unedited version of the report and believed there was "a strong circumstantial case." Lockyer said he would contact Carnaviera of the Attorney General's office to obtain permission for me to release the Pauline Dudley information to him. But before this happened, an inquiry was ordered in the Truscott case, to be overseen by Justice Fred Kaufman. Lockyer contacted Kaufman directly seeking permission for me to testify.

On January 17, I received a letter from Lockyer, along with a copy of the letter sent to Kaufman, advising him of my willingness to appear at the hearing and the fact that information Kaufman had received concerning Talbot was "incomplete." Subsequently, my lawyer received an e-mail from Mark Sandler of the law firm Cooper, Sandler and West in Toronto, advising me to appear at the inquiry on February 28. Sandler was the counsel assisting Kaufman at the inquiry and, because Kaufman was out of the country, Sandler was handling this part of the inquiry. Also, the inquiry was being held at the Cooper, Sandler and West offices.

Just before I started my testimony, I provided the inquiry with three reports:

a. "Submission to the Honourable Mr. Justice Kaufman in the Application under 690 of the Criminal Code in the Matter of Steven Truscott."[5]

This brief included:
1. Introduction
2. Larry Talbot: Criminal record.
3. Information linking Talbot to the Pauline Dudley homicide.
4. Information potentially linking Talbot to the Lynne Harper homicide.
5. Talbot as a suspect in the Harper Homicide — the rationale.
6. The Harper and Dudley Homicides — A Comparative Analysis.
7. The OPP Investigation of Talbot 1997-1999.
8. Summary of the OPP deficiencies in the investigation of Talbot as a suspect in the Harper and Dudley murders.
9. Other matters.
10. Concluding remarks.

b. "Copy of Original Notes Barry Ruhl (Ret. OPP) for the Honourable Mr. Justice Kaufman-690 Application." (December 26, 1997-April 10, 2000.)[6]

In a covering letter, I advised Kaufman the purpose of the journal was to document the conversations with OPP personnel and that immediately after each conversation, the journal notes had been entered into my computer. I also provided him with the rough notes I made before and during my conversations with the officers. In some cases, questions were written prior to speaking with the officer(s) while in others, I'd noted key words as we spoke.

c. "Suspect — Cheryl Lynne Harper Homicide — For The Honourable Mr. Justice Kaufman – 690 Application Barry Ruhl (Ret. OPP)

This précis was specifically related to the rationale for considering Talbot a person of interest in the Lynne Harper homicide and comparing it with the Pauline Dudley homicide.

On February 28, I appeared to testify with Sandler as counsel and he suggested I simply relate my story, as opposed to following a question and answer format.

My testimony addressed two issues: Larry Talbot and the homicide of Lynne Harper, and the investigation by the Ontario Provincial Police.

I discussed the encounters I had with Talbot; the Pauline Dudley homicide and Talbot; the Lynne Harper homicide and the circumstantial case; a comparison of the Harper and Dudley crime scenes and MO employed; and the OPP's investigation of Talbot. I was on the stand for two hours.

One of the few occasions Sandler interrupted was when I testified that Lynne Harper was included in the OPP Behavioural Sciences submission obtained by Lockyer, when he was preparing for the Inquiry. He said he didn't think she was but corrected himself after reviewing his material, which included three other victims and Lynne Harper.[7]

When I finally finished, Sandler thanked me and said he found the testimony "fascinating." He said he didn't know what Kaufman would do with the information, but speculated we may need to meet again. He also indicated he wanted to discuss some aspects of the information with Insp. Jeff McGuire, a Toronto Police inspector assisting at the inquiry.[8]

I felt a huge weight had been lifted from my chest after I left the law offices, partly because of all the hours I had put in preparing for the inquiry, but also because of the stress of criticizing the OPP, my former employer in a job I loved. But now it was a matter of public record.

According to Julian Sher, Kaufman interviewed 21 witnesses, including Steven Truscott, several people who were children in Clinton at the time of the murder, police officers, medical experts and two journalists, Sher himself, and research associate Theresa Burke.[9]

Among the witnesses were Arnold "Butch" George and Jacqueline Gaudet and "apparently (George) changed his story again and told yet another version of what happened — his fifth," Sher reported in an edition of his book updated in 2007. The testimony wasn't made public, but the Crown admitted it was "inconsistent" with what he said in court.[10]

Jocelyne Gaudet's evidence was "spotty at best," Sher said. She didn't remember Steven calling at her house on the evening of June 9, as the prosecutor alleged, nor could she say if she was looking for Lynne or Steve as she walked up and down the county road. She also complained about being awakened and questioned "without the presence of her father" in a room with three officers. She said "they kept trying to change my words" (without providing any specifics.) "Here's this twelve year old kid, half asleep, and these bastards are trying to change my story,"[11] she said.

Steven Truscott testified on August 2002 and March 2003. He essentially recounted his activities on the night of June 9, up to and including his arrest. Justice Kaufman asked Steven if "financial compensation" was a factor in asking the government to reopen the case. He said, "My main interest is clearing my name. I want my kids to go through life with a name they're proud of, not something that has a stigma attached to it."[12]

The Ontario Attorney General lawyers attempted to discredit him, suggesting his "version" of what happened to Lynne Harper on June 9, 1959 is not worthy of belief. They also mentioned his dismal performance at the Supreme Court, whose judges (excluding one) seemed unimpressed with his story.

But Justice Kaufman, "after reviewing the extensive record of Truscott's police statements, and the trial transcripts from 1959 and 1966, came down solidly in favor of Steven's credibility," Sher said.

"On the totality of the available evidence, Truscott's evidence on the critical events is not incapable of belief," Kaufman concluded.[13]

After the inquiry, Kaufman's 700-page report was submitted to Justice Minister Irwin Cotler in August 2004. Although some of it was not released, much of it proved very interesting. With regard to the recollection of civilian witnesses, "many of them children,"

Kaufman noted that none of the witnesses prepared their "own contemporaneous notes of the relevant events."

Their "recollections" were captured in original witness statements, "their accuracy was in part "dependent upon the objectivity and skill of the questioner ... Witnesses who are subjected to multiple interviews, particularly by the authorities may be susceptible to influences that shape and alter their memories ... They may tell the questioner what they think he or she wants to hear. Or the written statement may not reflect precisely what the witnesses said or thought. These concerns are particularly manifest where impressionable child witnesses are involved."[14]

The report indicated Kaufman also heard testimony of other possible suspects.

- Other sightings of strange cars on the evening of June 9.
- The case of Alexander Kalichuk, an airman who had tried to lure young girls into his car (in the St. Thomas area) and whose name was raised in the mid- '60s to OPP investigator Harold Graham, but was dismissed.
- A salesman (Talbot) who drove a 1957 Bel Air and later pled guilty to various crimes.
- A man with four convictions of assaulting females who allegedly told his doctor on his death bed he had "done the murder that Steven Truscott went to jail for."
- A military man at the base between 1958 and 1959 who was a member of the search party, but later, for some reason, felt the need to tell police he was "miles away."[15]

Sher said none of these possible other suspects necessarily proved a miscarriage of justice, but in Kaufman's mind they raised the specter of "tunnel vision" on the part of police and prosecutors. "This investigation — right or wrongly — focused on Truscott. Traditional police work such as the identification of local sexual offenders may not have been pursued with vigor, or not at all," Kaufman concluded.[16]

Kaufman spoke specifically about Talbot and my testimony but our names were redacted to maintain our anonymity. Redactions are indicated by use of brackets:

According to ( ) ( ) has a penchant for neatness. ( ) provided examples suggesting that ( ) crimes reflect this trait. ( ) also suggested that ( ) is a well-organized sexual predator whose penchant for carrying knives and hockey laces clearly illustrates the potential for violence upon the women he preyed. (sic)

> ( ) requested the opportunity to meet with me and Mr. Sandler to provide information concerning ( ). It is ( ) belief that ( ) should be investigated as the perpetrator in the Lynne Harper homicide and others. ( ) provided us with a great deal of information about ( ) and his alleged involvement in a series of homicides for which he had not been charged. It would appear that ( ) was regarded as a prime suspect by the Halton Regional Police (and apparently with good reason) in the homicide of a young woman who was hitchhiking at a location not far from where ( ) was admittedly parked. There are features of that unsolved murder that are similar to the Lynne Harper homicide. ( ) has raised Talbot's involvement in that homicide and others, including the Lynne Harper homicide, with the OPP and has expressed great dissatisfaction over the OPP's perceived reluctance to seriously consider ( ) as a suspect in the Harper case. He was examined by Mr. Sandler under oath on February 28, 2003. His views in this regard, and the evidence which he relies upon to support ( ) possible involvement in various homicides are contained in Appendix T and need not be reproduced here.[17]

Kaufman also said:

He was a salesman in southwestern Ontario. Although he denied ever attending the Canadian Air Force base, there is some evidence that the salesman who took over his route was required to attend several times a year.

Kaufman also addressed "disclosure rules," which were almost non-existent in 1959. In other words, there wasn't an obligation for the Crown to release evidence to Steven's lawyers. He said the non-disclosure of key evidence by the Crown "deprived the defence of a considerable amount of information that could have been used to impeach the credibility of witnesses, cast doubt upon the prosecution's theory of the case, or support the defence case. In some instances, the evidence would have made it possible to discover and explore new avenues of investigation. This undisclosed evidence . . . could reasonably be expected to have affected the verdict," the justice concluded, and "contribute to a reasonable basis for concluding that there was a likely miscarriage of justice."

There was no mention in the media of the testimony I had given, and while Kaufman's conclusions were encouraging, his recommendations to the justice minister were not known.

Like Steven Truscott, his family, and his supporters, I waited for a decision.

CHAPTER 9

LAST CHANCE FOR JUSTICE

The headline on October 29, 2004, in the *Globe and Mail* said it in just two words: "Justice Delayed." Justice Minister Irwin Cotler "bounced Steven Truscott's 45-year-old murder conviction back to the Ontario Court of Appeal. Cotler said "there was a miscarriage of justice in this case", but the only appropriate remedy was to have the appeal court review the evidence, the newspaper reported. The decision meant it would be years before the case would be heard.[1]

Steven accepted the news with an air of optimism, "They had sentenced me to death once, so anything else is a plus. ... I'll be vindicated. It will just take longer."[2]

The appeal began June 19, 2006, at the Ontario Court of Appeal in Toronto. Steven was represented by James Lockyer, Phil Campbell and Marlys Edwardth. For three weeks, medical, scientific, and witness testimony was presented. Unlike previous trials, the court heard only fresh evidence.

Experts testifying for Truscott's lawyers included:

Dr. Michael Pollanen, Ontario forensic pathologist:

. . . Stomach contents suggest a time of death closer to the evening or the night of June 9, 1959, but the state of the body, histology and weather suggest a time of death more towards the day or night of June 10, 1959.[3]

- Dr. Nicholas Diamand, University of Toronto:

It is not possible to define exact time of death or even time of death based on any examination of stomach contents. One may say that the state of stomach contents is consistent or compatible with death having occurred within a particular time period. However, the possible time of death cannot be limited to that period on the basis of stomach contents alone. ... Stomach contents (are) not useless or discredited, but it is of limited value and without precision. ... Dr. Penistan could not use the state of Lynne Harper's stomach content to limit the time of death to one or two hours after her last meal. ... In the case of Lynne Harper, the state of the stomach contents was compatible with death having occurred one or two hours after she finished her meal, but it cannot be limited to that time period.[4]

Dr. Bernard Knight, professor emeritus at the University of Wales and a fellow of the Royal College of Pathologists, who said he had performed "between 25, 000 and 30,000 autopsies" in his career, and was the author of a number of texts, including Knights Forensic Pathology:

An estimate of the time of death based on the volume of stomach contents and state of digestion should never be used as probative evidence: it could perhaps be used to direct the police investigation,

but you cannot pin it down to any useful period of
time in pinpointing the time of death.[5]

The justices at the appeal were critical of testimony by Crown
witness Dr. Werner Spitz, who provided the opinion that Lynne
Harper died by 7:45 p.m. and called Penistan's original findings
"admirably accurate" and said they rest on "solid scientific founda-
tion." It became clear during cross-examination, however, that the
only basis for Dr. Spitz's opinion was his own experience in conducting autopsies and his belief that if stomach contents are readily
identifiable at autopsy, then death must have occurred within two
hours of the last meal. "In the result, we have not placed any reli-
ance on his evidence and we give it no further mention," the justices said.[6]

Entomology or bug evidence was also introduced at the hearing.
In 1959, the science of forensic entomology had not developed
enough to assist in solving the murder of Lynne Harper. Yet by
good fortune, two events contributed to create factual data that
arguably now permit the modern science of forensic entomology to
shed some light on the time of Lynne Harper's death[7]:

One was that insect maggots and eggs were collected by Dr.
Penistan from Harper's body, at the crime scene and during the
autopsy. The second was that the samples were sent to the attorney general's laboratory, where Dr. Elgin Brown reared the larvae
samples and identified the specimens. Fifty years later, his findings
provided "raw material for opinions by entomology experts on the
time of Harper's death.[8] Two scientists testifying for Truscott's team
agreed that the entomological evidence suggested a time of death
much later than originally claimed. A dissenting witness called by
the Crown to support the original findings was seen as "dogmatic
and reluctant to admit obvious errors", and was termed "adversarial"
by the justices, who did not find his testimony credible.[9]

The justices concluded that "broadly speaking, all of the experts
whose opinions were placed before the court except one offered
at least some support for the appellant's claim that Lynne died
hours after 8 p.m. on June 9 and probably sometime the following morning.

There were also witnesses from the Clinton area, as well as OPP officer Harry (Hank) Sayeau, who had assisted Graham in the original investigation. Sayeau, according to Sher, couldn't explain why he dismissed statements from two key witnesses that contradicted the Crown's case:

Karen Daum was a nine-year-old who was hunting turtles with Dougie Oates the night Lynne disappeared and told police "she saw Steve and Lynne on his bike close to the river."

But Sayeau noted: "She was a cute little girl but she had to be wrong. She's not credible as far as the crown was concerned."[10]

Daryl Wadsworth remembered seeing Steven Truscott leave the schoolyard at about 7:25 p.m., much later than the Crown's theory that Truscott set off on his bike ride closer to 7 p.m. Sayeau characterized Daryl's evidence as "imaginative. Wouldn't consider his story at all."[11]

Sayeau testified at the appeal that none of the OPP detachments in the area were contacted about a possible child rapist or sexual predator in the vicinity. He said he had never heard of Alexander Kalichuk, the heavy-drinking airman who tried to lure young girls into his car two weeks before Lynne was murdered. Justice Michael Moldaver asked Sayeau why the police never considered a sexual psychopath might be responsible for Lynne's rape and murder before they narrowed their focus on a 14-year-old:

"Did the thought ever cross your mind that, for someone to … strangle her, then sexually assault her, you might want to be looking for someone who is more of a pervert, more of a sexual psychopath? Did you ever talk about that with your colleagues?"

"I don't recall that," said Sayeau, 84 at the time of the appeal.[12]

In *The Trial of Steven Truscott*, Isabel LeBourdais said:

> All the evidence indicated that she was attacked after dark by moonlight, in an unknown spot, by an older man who had a psychotic personality and plenty of time — not in broad daylight in Lawson's Bush by a fourteen-year-old boy who was quite normal and had very little time indeed.[13]

Bob Lawson, owner of Lawson's bush, testified he saw a mysterious red convertible parked near the bush late Tuesday evening but the police weren't interested because they had already arrested Truscott. He also said Gaudet came to him during the trial to ask him to change his testimony. She had testified she had come by his farm looking for Steve around 6:30 p.m. when in fact the farmer knew it was closer to an hour later, around 7:30 p.m.[14]

Sandra Stolzmann testified Gaudet told her in the 1960s that she had lied at the trial. They were nursing students in Montreal when the Supreme Court decided to hear Truscott's appeal. "They've got the wrong guy, they've got the wrong guy," Gaudet kept repeating.[15]

Catherine Beaman was the only witness to testify about Lynne's "propensity to hitchhike." She was almost the same age as Lynne and said they were good friends. She testified that it was common for children of their age to hitchhike in the area. In her words, "It was just a way of life." Beaman testified she could recall hitchhiking with Lynne at least 15 or 20 times.[16]

Truscott's lawyers suggested that there were other potential suspects in the case including Larry Talbot. He was referred to as "a man identified by a retired OPP detective as a possible suspect in several homicides, including the murder of Lynne Harper."

Their presentation regarding Talbot was as follows:

> Retired Detective Barry Ruhl had personally been the victim of a night-time burglary by this suspect and was shot by him with a pellet gun as he pursued him. The retired officer, who knew of Lynne's murder and the controversy surrounding the Appellant's (Truscott's) conviction, conducted his own investigation of the man and reported his findings to the OPP. He also testified before Justice Kaufman.
>
> The suspect in 1959 was a salesman in southwestern Ontario. He made sales stops several times each year at the Air Force base in Clinton and drove a 1957 Bel Air. The analysis and investigative work

of the retired detective is extensive. He submitted his report to the OPP with a covering letter which said: The enclosed report considers the possibility that the above suspect is responsible for one or more homicides of young women in Ontario including the murder of Lynne Harper in 1959. The passage of time makes it effectively impossible to recreate the movements of this man on June 9, 1959. If, however, the police investigating Lynne's murder had undertaken the obvious task of cross-referencing Chevrolet owners in southwestern Ontario, this man could have been identified and his whereabouts established at that time.

The information disclosed by the OPP includes the following analysis from a detective (in the Behavioural Science Unit):

There are some similarities in the cases involving (three named female murder victims) and Lynne Harper. These include similar ages (Harper was younger) similar physical appearance (white females with long hair), all victims hitchhiked, all were transported significant distances, the most probable motivation in each case was sexual assault, all were disposed of or had clothes found in areas considered lover's lanes. Cause of death could not be determined in many cases due to decomposition.

Some features common in known serial killers are also present in (the suspect's) background. These included but are not limited to the following:

Male, white
Working class
Engages in stalking behaviour
Highly mobile covering large geographic areas
Lack of empathy for their victims

Deviant sexual behaviour
Anti-social personality features
Social isolation
History of violent behaviour
Manipulative and cunning
Lack of remorse
Parental abuse or neglect

(The suspect) has deviant sexual interests. This
had been demonstrated by his actions of: prowling
around residences at night and peeking in windows;
carrying a rape kit (tape, mask, Vaseline, dildo,
knives, pellet gun, house breaking tools); pointing the gun at a victim and insisting she raise her
nightgown; frequenting strip clubs in Buffalo; and
cruising alone late at night in areas known as lover's
lanes. While under surveillance he was observed
attempting to pick up hitchhikers.

Conclusion

(The suspect) presents himself as a viable suspect for
the murder of (a named female victim). (The detective's) extensive background on (the suspect) raises
concerns that (the suspect) may be responsible for
one or more homicides. We do not believe him to
be responsible for all the cases identified. However,
we believe a review of the cases is warranted to
ascertain what evidence is still available and to
establish if any connection can be made between
(the suspect) and the murders of (three named
female victims), Lynne Harper or others.

When this man was questioned on September 27,
2000, he denied involvement in Lynne's murder and
said that he had never been on the Air Force base,
though he had a cousin who resided in Clinton.
The questioning was superficial and there is no

indication that he has been further investigated, nor that his claim that he had never been at the base which contradicts other information available to the OPP has been verified or examined.[17]

Regarding Talbot, lawyers for the Crown countered that this was information "not known to anyone until well after 1959."

Aside from suspicion and an attempt at "profiling," there does not appear to be anything connecting this individual to any of the murders alleged, let alone the murder of Lynne Harper. No evidence has been proffered as to the appearance of a 1957 Chevrolet Bel Air. In any event, what the Appellant proposes that the police should have done in 1959 is unfathomable. The Appellant has proffered no evidence relating to the 'ease' with which this could have been done. There can be little doubt that in 1959 in southwestern Ontario alone, there were thousands of owners of Chevrolet vehicles of various years and models. It is the Appellant's view that each of these owners should have been located and their movements ascertained. It is not clear that had they even performed this Herculean task, this particular individual would even have come to their attention. This is the "CSI Effect" with the benefit of time travel.[18]

The Crown also argued that other potential suspects were investigated:

> The Appellant concedes that the search for "other
> suspects" has not located anyone to this day.
> Nevertheless, he advances several alleged "potential
> suspects" as candidates. All of these candidates have
> been investigated. None has been linked in any way
> to the murder of Lynne Harper. Much of the infor-
> mation relied upon by the Appellant could not have
> come to the attention of the police in 1959, because
> it did not exist or occur until after the Appellant's
> conviction. None of the information in any way
> supports the allegation that the police deliberately
> refused to investigate information, leads or tips that
> came to their attention.[19]

James Lockyer countered that the questioning of Talbot was superficial "and there is no indication that he has been further investigated, nor that his claim that he had never been at the base, which contradicts other information available to the OPP, has been verified or examined."[20]

In the end, the justices concluded none of the evidence of other suspects "should be brought to bear on our analysis of the appropriate remedy in this case. The information is too speculative and inconclusive to give it any weight in deciding what remedy the appellant is entitled to in these proceedings."[21] But at the conclusion of the hearing, they enumerated the factors they did find relevant:

> We are satisfied that the fresh evidence and the new material before this court have significantly undermined the strength of each of the four factual pillars of the Crown's case. In contrast, much of that material has given added force to the evidentiary foundation of the defense case.[22]

> First, on the crucial issue of the time of Lynne Harper's death, the pathology evidence that we have admitted as fresh evidence renders the expert medical evidence heard in the prior judicial proceedings, to the effect that Lynne must have died before 8 p.m. on June 9, scientifically untenable.[23]

> Entomology evidence that could well be received at a new trial further undermines the Crown's claim that Lynne Harper died before 8 p.m.[24]

> Archival material suggests that a credible case could be made that Philip Burns and Richard Gellatly did not leave the area of the bridge at the same time and proceed in tandem southbound on the County Road. Instead, the material suggests that Burns left several minutes before Gellatly. This would explain why Gellatly saw the appellant and Lynne and Burns did not.[25]

At the trial, the Crown alleged both Richard Gellatly and Philip Burns left the bridge at the same time heading back to the base. Gellatly was riding his bike and testified he passed Steven and Lynne south of Lawson's Bush. Philip Burns testified that when he was walking back to the base, he didn't see them. The Crown argued since Gellatly saw them biking south of Lawson's Bush and Burns didn't, they must have gone into the bush. The Crown introduced two witnesses, Donna Dunkin and Bev Geiger, who were at the bridge and testified the boys left the bridge at the same time. Gellatly riding his bike and Burns walking.[26] The justices continued:

> The Crown's post-offence conduct rested principally on the testimony of Arnold George and on photographic evidence suggesting that the appellant could not possibly have seen the details of a car at the highway from his position on the bridge. The archival material is capable of seriously undermining George's credibility to the extent that a jury would be unlikely to act on his evidence standing alone.[27]

> The archival and photographic material also indicates that the evidence relied on by the Crown at trial to show that the appellant could not see the details of a vehicle from his vantage point on the bridge was highly misleading. This material provides support for the claim that the appellant could reasonably believe that he saw the color of the license plate on the vehicle while standing on the bridge.[28]

> The penis lesions evidence that so vividly demonstrated the appellant's guilt at trial had been weakened to the extent that is virtually no evidence at all.[29]

Following this summation, the justices delivered their decision:

> We have concluded that, while it cannot be said that no jury acting judicially could reasonably convict, we are satisfied that if a new trial were possible, an

acquittal would clearly be the more likely result. Having regard to the highly unusual circumstances of this Reference, we have determined that the most appropriate remedy is to enter an acquittal. Accordingly, in the words of s.696.3 (3) (ii) of the Criminal Code, the appeal is allowed.[30]

A smiling Steven Truscott on the front page of the *London Free Press* on August 29, 2007 said it all.

"The long journey for vindication finally arrived," the newspaper reported. "The man at the centre of one of the most controversial legal dramas in Canadian history no longer is a convicted murderer — acquitted yesterday in a historic decision by the Ontario Court of Appeal. 'We are satisfied that Mr. Truscott's conviction was a miscarriage of justice and must be quashed,' the judges said."[31]

The same day, the *National Post* published a story saying "OPP could re-open search for 1959 killer." Then OPP Commissioner Julian Fantino was quoted as saying:

There's challenges here to try and go back to a case that's 40 years old . . . We'll address all of that. We'll do what needs to be done and ensure that we fulfill our responsibility to the extent that we can with whatever evidence is available.

Fantino said the OPP planned to meet with the attorney general's office to review Truscott's appeal court acquittal and discuss whether the force should commit fresh resources to solving Harper's murder. He also made favourable comments about Graham's team: "Those [officers] were honorable in what they did and I believe they tried to do the honest, right thing."[32]

On July 7, 2008, the Ontario government awarded Steven $6.5 million and Attorney General Michael Bryant offered an apology. Truscott wasn't impressed. "I know he apologized on behalf of the government but I don't really feel the apology was sincere."[33]

As for me, I was hoping the OPP would reopen the case, but that didn't happen. It was time to walk away. Then, Talbot re-entered our lives in a way we could never have imagined.

CHAPTER 10

LAST CALL

On Friday, June 27, 2008, the phone at our home rang but when my wife Pat answered, there was no one on the line. We have call display so she dialed the number and a male with a raspy voice answered. "Oh hello," Pat said. "Somebody just called here from that number."

The person responded with an "Oh, oh!" and hung up. She thought it must have been a wrong number. The next day when the phone rang, Pat answered it again.

Pat: "Hello."

Caller: "Is Barry there?"

Pat: "No he isn't, he just went to the gym."

Caller: "Are you the girl from 40 years ago?"

Pat: "who is this?"

Caller: "Never mind, but if you're the girl from 40 years ago, I want to apologize to you and have some nice things to say to you, but not some nice things to say to Barry. I see he writes a lot in the *Toronto Star*."

Pat realized, to her horror, that it was Talbot on the line, but she managed to keep her composure.

Pat: "Well, Barry should be home from the gym no later than five o'clock. If you call, you'll get him then."

Talbot: "OK, I'll call back today or tomorrow. I'm using a cell phone because I'm in the hospital and it's too expensive to call out."

When Talbot hung up, Pat called the gym.

Pat: "You'll never guess who just called?"

Me: "Who?"

Pat: "Larry Talbot."

Me: "You're kidding! I'll be right home. Write down what he said, and if he calls back, don't pick up."

This was an unwelcome intrusion, and why then? I wondered if it had something to do with a *Toronto Star* article — "Other leads on possible suspects" — written almost a year earlier by Tracey Tyler, about the Truscott case. In it she mentioned:

> ... a former salesman who drove a 1957 Chevy and apparently called at the Clinton base frequently. The man came to police attention after he tried to break into the home of retired OPP Det. Barry Ruhl, who shot him with a pellet gun and began his own investigation. In a report to the OPP, Ruhl concluded the man could be a potential suspect in several murders, including Lynne's.[1]

Unfortunately, the reporter had part of it wrong — Talbot shot me. Nevertheless, I speculated that the article may have caused anxiety for Talbot if he was responsible for the murder of Lynne, or any of the women mentioned in my report. Did he wonder what I knew? Did he worry the cops would pay him another visit? Or was the purpose of the call to try to obtain information? My imagination ran wild.

When I arrived home, Pat said she had been playing detective. She had called a hospital near where Talbot lived and asked for him. He wasn't there but when she called another one in the area, she discovered he was a patient there.

I phoned a friend who was a psychologist, and he theorized Talbot might have called to apologize. He suggested I record the conversation if Talbot called again, but also suggested Talbot might "shut down" if I mentioned the Harper killing.

I considered my friend's theory, but still wondered why now, 37 years after the cottage invasion and, coincidentally or not, following the vindication of Steven Truscott.

Also, Talbot's words to Pat and my friend's theory raised an interesting contradiction in terms of the characteristics attributed to Talbot at the Kaufman Inquiry by the Behavioural Sciences Unit.[2]

> Some features common in known serial killers
> are also present in (the suspect's) background …
> (including) lack of empathy for their victims, anti-
> social personality features (and) lack of remorse.

I called General Headquarters in Orillia to report the call from Talbot and on July 1, two detective constables, Gord Johnston and Mel Joa of the South Bruce OPP, came to our residence. We discussed the call and they recorded my account of my involvement with Talbot. It began at 9:16 p.m. and concluded at 10:31 p.m. I included information about the reports submitted to the OPP and the disappointing results. The officers also obtained a statement from Pat. Johnston said he'd call the next day and we were impressed with their interest and enthusiasm.

The following day, Johnston called and said his supervisors were considering a wiretap to record the conversation in case Talbot called. Joa thought it would also be a good idea if Pat and I completed a ViCLAS questionnaire regarding the break in at the cottage. These documents are stored in a database at OPP General Headquarters and are used to compare crimes with similar characteristics.

Detective Johnson contacted Det. Sgt. Jim Van Allen, manager of the OPP Criminal Profiling and a certified profiler. He had several recommendations about how I should handle the conversation if I spoke to Talbot:

- Ask what he wants to talk about.
- Sex offenders think differently, and Talbot might actually have a lot of respect for me.
- Be accepting and not authoritative or superior.

- Be flexible and open — for example, ask if there is anyone else he wants to speak to or ask what I can do for him.
- Mention we share a long history.
- If I ask questions about Harper, it's important to tell Talbot I'm not asking for the cops but for Truscott and just need a little information to help him out.

We were told a technician would contact us to install the wire.

I was pessimistic that a conversation with Talbot would yield any information and I didn't think Talbot would give up anything on the Harper killing (if he was responsible). On the other hand, we had nothing to lose.

On July 2, the GHQ duty officer advised Det. Insp. Chris Gilpin of CIB had been assigned to the case. I thought about the previous investigations and wondered if it would be different this time. On July 3, Gilpin met us and advised I'd be seen as an "agent" and the "wire" would be an unlawful interception. However, I could speak to Talbot and Gilpin could listen.

I was nervous prior to calling Talbot, but in a sense, I was now the predator and he was the prey. Questions were running through my head as I dialed: Could I pull it off? What if he hangs up? What if he confesses?

Talbot: "Hello"

Me: "Is that you Larry? It's Barry Ruhl."

Talbot: "Hi."

Me: "What are you doing in the hospital?"

Talbot: "I've got COPD (Chronic Obstructive Pulmonary Disease) — too much smoking for a long time."

Me: "So what have you been up to?"

Talbot: "I've been retired for almost 20 years and still with my wife. We've been together for almost 50 years. I called your place because I wanted to apologize to the woman if she was the same one from 1970."

Me: "Yeah she is."

Talbot: "She's okay, but you're a cop!" (laughing)

Me: "So Pat tells me you had something bad to say about me."

Talbot: "I'm upset at an article in the paper that didn't mention my name but mentioned a travelling salesman with a 1957 Chevy frequented the Clinton Air Force Base on business. I've never been on that base in my life. Why did you write this?"

Me: "What are you, a cop?" (We both laughed)

Talbot: "Yeah, I've read other articles you wrote. I feel sorry for Truscott. Had a tea party sitting around the kitchen with my wife and a couple of policewomen talking to me about Lynne Harper. They asked me a few questions like have you been to Clinton? One time I had two cops coming around to question me about the murder of two women from the Palgrave area. They thought I was armed. And instead of being quiet about this, they went to my place of business and also checked records I kept in my house to see where I'd been travelling."

Me: "Yeah, I know the cases you're talking about. An ex metro cop was convicted of the murders."

Talbot: "Oh. I found out where you lived from a friend, who looked you up on the internet. Yeah, and what I did was a childish prank."

Me: "All forgiven, but you sure packed a mean wallop and shot me!"

Talbot: "It probably didn't go in too far and you gave me a couple of good shots as well. (Both laughed.)

Talbot (cont'd): "Yeah, I was thinking of what I wore that night and could have improved on that. (laughing.) I lost my job after that."

Me: "I'm thinking that maybe I could drop in and pay you a visit as we head up your way when we go to our cottage in the Parry Sound area."

Talbot: "Fine, I'm the only Larry Talbot in the phone book."

Me: "How's the food in the hospital?"

Talbot: "It's okay. But not many people visit me."

Me: "No, me neither since I retired."

Talbot: "Oh by the way, I had my record expunged."

Me: "Oh. OK Larry. Got to go. It was good talking to you, and I may give you another call. Take care."

Talbot: "Good talking to you. Goodbye."

The *Toronto Star* article Talbot mentioned to
Pat Ruhl when he called June 28, 2008.

I discussed the surreal conversation with Gilpin and Joa, and we agreed the *Toronto Star* article had upset him, but only momentarily because he didn't stay on topic and laughed when I responded with: "What are you, a cop?"

I found it interesting that he mentioned reading "other articles" I had written. Most were letters to the editor published in the *Toronto Star*, and one was about Truscott. He referred to the interview with Schwantz as a "tea party" and didn't appear to have been upset about it.

Pat and Barry Ruhl April 2014.

It was clear Talbot was going to be difficult to investigate, and Gilpin suggested we try to get him to take a polygraph examination. This was an appropriate strategy because there wasn't any physical evidence from the Harper homicide, and he had previously volunteered to take a polygraph test in connection with the Dudley homicide.

Gilpin was going to contact Halton Regional Police to ascertain if hair found in Talbot's vehicle had been kept. She was also going to retrieve the files at General Headquarters pertaining to Talbot. She discovered they had been destroyed, and I gave her files I had. She mentioned Talbot had been caught recently making obscene phone calls, but didn't elaborate. Subsequently, she told me Talbot was charged with stealing his neighbour's telephone services so he could call porn sites. He was charged with theft of services and received a conditional discharge.

I suggested a ViCLAS examination to compare the Harper and Dudley homicides, but she said she didn't have any success with it and preferred the DNA analysis process. I didn't question her, but knew there was no DNA remaining from the Harper case, so I assumed she was referring to the Dudley homicide or other cold cases.

On July 5, Joa called and wanted us to complete a ViCLAS questionnaire. The *OPP Review* — Winter 2007/08 explained the purpose of the program:

> Since January 2007, ViCLAS has potentially linked
> 152 Ontario cases through behavioural analysis.
> In relation to those cases, 23 were confirmed
> links involving sexual assaults and one case was a
> confirmed link to a homicide. ViCLAS identified
> the unknown offender in each of these cases based
> upon the verbal, physical and sexual behaviour
> exhibited by the offenders in previous known
> offender submissions.[3]

For example, when Talbot placed an object against the door to ensure an unhampered exit, that MO would be noted in the ViCLAS database for comparison with other crime scenes.

On July 16, our questionnaires were entered in the database. Gilpin also wanted my input on the Christine Prince and Delia Adriano homicides, as well as credit card transactions from Talbot's account and information on the sexual assault of the young girl at Wasaga Beach. I met Joa at the Kincardine Detachment on July 19 and discussed the following:

- The sexual assault of the girl at Wasaga Beach.
- Talbot's MasterCard account – 20 gas purchases in 1982.
- An intelligence report forwarded to Criminal Intelligence Ontario on September 23, 1982 with information on Talbot.
- Journal notes of my interview with Les Church.
- Journal notes of the Christine Prince homicide.
- Chronology of offences involving Talbot.
- Newspaper articles about Christine Prince and Delia Adriano.

- Report resulting in Project Tree (March 15, 1983.)
- Intelligence report-District Seven (August 6, 1981) Larry Talbot-"Suspect For Observation."

I also included information about a homicide on September 1, 1990 at Cumberland Beach, near Orillia. It involved the rape and murder of 13-year-old Leah Sousa and the severe beating of her mother Lora:

> At approximately 10:30 a.m. on September 1, 1990, Leah Sousa was found by her friend in the backyard of her residence at 281 Beachview Avenue, Cumberland Beach, just north of Orillia. Investigators believe that Leah Sousa was asleep on the living room sofa when the initial attack on her took place. Leah's mother Lora was found injured, but alive, at the scene. Investigators have been able to determine that the attack on Lora Sousa began in the bedroom. Lora somehow managed to get into the living room where she was further attacked. Leah was assaulted and struck about the head several times while she was lying on the couch. Entry to the home was gained through the rear door by breaking one of the panes of glass in the door and then reaching in and unlocking the door. Once inside, the culprit(s) located the victims and began to brutally attack them. ...Crime scene examination has led the police to believe that the culprit was wearing Men's size 9-10 Nike all-weather court shoes.[4]

I became aware of this case on April 30, 1992, at a Community Policing Meeting at Cumberland Beach. These meetings gave the police an opportunity to listen to concerns from area residents. When I was speaking to the community service officer, she mentioned the Sousa case and said the perpetrator gained entry by smashing a window pane in the rear door. Immediately I thought about Talbot, who used the same MO at our cottage. The Sousa residence was close to Highway 11 and Talbot lived approximately 30 minutes north of it. I compared the crimes:

- Both were committed after dark.
- Both gained entry by smashing a window pane in the rear door.
- Both attacks occurred after the victims were asleep.
- Both attacks were sexually motivated.
- Leah, Lora and I were beaten about the head.
- The suspect wore a size 9-10 running shoe. Talbot wore a size 9 running shoe.
- Talbot would be familiar with Cumberland Beach.
- (There was other relevant information given to Gilpin.)

On May 5, 1992, I gave the information to the Seven District Headquarters Crime Unit but don't know if any follow-up was done.

On September 28, 2008, Joa told us Gilpin would be coming to our residence the next day. That night I had difficulty sleeping, as a myriad of thoughts swirled around in my head. I knew Gilpin had met with Toronto and Halton Regional Police and figured Christine Prince, Delia Adriano and Pauline Dudley were probably the cold cases under review. I also knew Gilpin had spent a considerable time on the investigation. But had she been successful?

On September 29, many of my questions were answered, but not in the way I'd hoped. Gilpin informed us:

- None of the physical evidence in the Dudley case, including hair and blood, was retained by Halton Regional Police.
- There wasn't any forensic evidence in the Prince homicide.
- Two cold cases in Toronto were reviewed but the DNA profile didn't match Talbot.
- There wasn't any physical evidence at the Cindy Halliday crime scene.
- The file of the young girl at Wasaga Beach had been destroyed.
- There were two cold cases in the Midland and Barrie area, but they were too recent considering Talbot's age.
- Gilpin believed Talbot was responsible for a number of crimes other than those he was suspected of committing.

Then came the worst news of all. Gilpin said Talbot had passed away in a nursing home on September 8, six days before Gilpin and investigators from Toronto and Halton Regional Police had planned to visit him.

We will never know what the outcome of that interview or any subsequent investigation of Talbot might have revealed. The answers to so many questions died with him.

But, Gilpin didn't stop making inquiries about Talbot. On May 27, 2009, I received a call from her and she had reviewed the murder of two women in the Thunder Bay area in 1972 but the MO wasn't similar to Talbot's. She also told me Joa had spoken to Talbot's sister following his death, to ascertain if she could shed any light on his criminal activities. (His sister had been forthcoming with the parole officer in 1979, when she suspected he broke into the cottage he recently sold, but nothing was learned from her.) But, she told Joa she believed there had been something wrong with him and he needed help. During the call, I asked Gilpin to consider storing his DNA in the databank, at the Centre of Forensic Sciences and she was going to check with her supervisor. I also asked her about the possibility of a ViCLAS analysis, comparing the Harper and Dudley homicides. She said she had thought about it, but didn't think the two cases were "close," and believed Truscott killed Lynne Harper. I also thought Truscott was guilty at one time, but I was surprised the decision by the Ontario Court of Appeal in 2007 hadn't changed her opinion.

I thanked Gilpin and Joa and told Gilpin it was unfortunate she hadn't been involved in the previous investigation. It might have resulted in a different outcome.

On April 30, 2010, Gilpin said she had received permission to include the files pertaining to Talbot in a tracking system capable of comparing crimes Talbot was suspected of committing with cold cases in the database.

Later on that year, I asked her to make sure Talbot was investigated for the Sousa homicide. Gilpin learned he had been investigated, but was eliminated as a suspect, and "No reason was provided." She was going to request a DNA analysis. On May 12, 2011, Gilpin was told a DNA analysis couldn't be completed. She said she would continue to monitor the Talbot file and contact me if anything was discovered. It was a very disappointing finale.

CHAPTER 11

A VIABLE SUSPECT
BEYOND REACH

There was jubilation when Steven Truscott was liberated from years of injustice, but in regards to the murder of Lynne Harper and the other potential or probable crimes committed by Larry Talbot, there is a lot of unfinished business.

The theories put forth that Talbot might have been responsible for a number of unsolved homicides and should have been more thoroughly investigated were not dismissed by many in the legal community. Lawyer Edward Greenspan and his associate, Todd White, said after reading my report that they believed there was "a strong circumstantial case" against Talbot in the Harper murder. Even the OPP Behavioural Sciences Unit recommended Talbot be investigated.

The Pauline Ivy Dudley homicide was the cornerstone of my hypothesis, and at the conclusion of the inquiry into the Truscott case, Justice Fred Kaufman remarked:

It would appear that (Talbot) was regarded as a prime suspect by the Halton Regional Police — and apparently with good reason — in the homicide of a young woman who was hitchhiking at a location not far from where (Talbot) was admittedly parked. There are features of that unsolved murder that are similar to the Lynne Harper homicide.[1]

The following is a comparative analysis of the known facts in the Harper and Dudley homicides:[2]

Cheryl Lynne Harper	Pauline Ivy Dudley
Hitchhiking	Hitchhiking
Tuesday evening	Tuesday evening
Lawson's Bush	Henderson Park
Partially naked	Partially naked
Pants removed	Pants removed
Neat crime scene	Neat crime scene
Shoes next to body	Shoes next to body
Underpants 33 feet from scene	Jean jacket 35 feet from scene
Two crime scenes	Two crime scenes
Tree branches on body	Pine branches/grass on body
Strangled	Strangled
Talbot customers in area	Talbot lived in Burlington (15 min. from scene)

In *Profiling Violent Crimes*, Ronald M. Holmes and Stephen T. Holmes suggest an offender's personality can't be altered:

> So it is with the criminal personality. It has taken years to become the person he now is. He will not, over a short period, radically change. It is not simply a matter of not wanting to change. He is not able to change. This assumption has fundamental importance to the profiling process. The inability to change will result in the perpetrator committing a similar crime in a similar fashion. Not only will the criminal commit the same crime but he may force

the victim to act out a scenario that he has also forced previous victims to perform.[3]

Authors, including Isabel LeBourdais, commented on the neatness of the crime scene, in *The Trial of Steven Truscott*:

> The outstanding feature of the scene in Lawson's Bush was its orderliness. This was not a man who tossed his victim into a ditch by the road or even hid her body in some swamp or thicket, miles away where it might not be found for weeks or months. Everything had to be tidy.[4]

Julian Sher described the crime scene in *Until You Are Dead*:

> What was surprising was the neat, almost ceremonial appearance of the scene. The leaves and earth around Lynne's body were undisturbed — no piles of dirt, scraped earth or broken branches to suggest a violent struggle. Her shoes and socks lay in a "fairly orderly manner." The police noted the white socks carefully rolled up. Her underwear had no rips or tears. Her shorts were zipped, no tears or cuts, just a slight rent in the seam near the crotch.[5]

I observed Talbot's penchant for neatness when I searched his vehicle following the break in at our cottage. This was also noted when the Oakville police opened his trunk and recorded it was "very tidy." When Talbot broke into another cottage at Sauble Beach, he placed a large towel on the bed and the investigating officer remarked: "Everything that had been disturbed by the intruder when he broke in had either been placed back in its original place or cleaned up." In my 30 years of investigations, I never encountered another tidy thief.

In *Profiling Violent Crimes*, Holmes and Holmes addressed an obsessive-compulsive behaviour in a personality type referred to as the "organized non-social offender":

> He has an organized personality that is reflected in his lifestyle, home, vehicle and personal appearance.

This kind of offender may be called an anal personality type; in his life, there is a place for everything
and everything must be in its place.[6]

The authors identified a list of characteristics
organized, non-social offenders may possess in "The
Holmes Typology" (Part 1)[7] Where information
is known, I have compared their list with Talbot
in brackets.

- IQ above average, 105-120 range. Unknown.
- Socially adequate. (Co-worker Bill Elliott called Talbot
  very personable.)
- Lives with partner. (Talbot was married for a lengthy period.)
- High birth order. Unknown.
- Stable father figure. (Talbot's father was an accountant.)
- Family physical abuse, harsh. (Talbot's father beat him with
  a cane.)
- Geographically/occupationally mobile. (Talbot was a travel-
  ling salesman.)
- Follows the news media. (Talbot made it clear in his com-
  ments to me that he was a newspaper reader.)
- May be college educated. (No, Grade 10.)
- Good hygiene/housekeeping skills. (Talbot's tendency toward
  neatness already noted. He also was observed well dressed and
  well groomed at court.)
- Does not usually keep a hiding place. Unknown.
- Daytime habits. Unknown.
- Drives a flashy car. (1957 Chevrolet 210 Bel Air)
- Returns to crime scene. (He received a speeding ticket
  on County Road 22, leading to the location where Cindy
  Halliday's body was discovered.)
- Usually contacts police to play games. (Unknown, but he did
  contact me and didn't seem fazed by contacts with police,
  based on his stated reaction to the Schwantz interview,
  for example.)
- A police groupie or wannabe. Unknown.

- Doesn't experiment with self-help. Unknown.
- Kills at one site, disposes at another. (This was the case in the Pauline Dudley homicide.)
- May dismember body. Unknown, but not a feature of any of the homicides I looked at.
- Attacks using seduction (and) restraints. Unknown, but he did have four sets of hockey laces with him when he invaded our cottage and surgical tape when he was investigated for the Dudley homicide.
- Keeps personal, holds a conversation. (His last conversation with me is evidence of that.)
- Leaves a controlled crime scene. (The Dudley crime scene could be called "controlled.")
- Leaves little physical evidence. (Again, the Dudley crime scene suggests this trait and this could explain why he was dismissed as a suspect in other cases.)
- Responds best to direct interview. Unknown, since neither Schwantz's interview nor my conversation with Talbot could be called probative.)

When I interviewed Les Church, Talbot's former co-worker, he said that when Talbot was under a great deal of stress or pressure, something came over him and he committed the crimes. A theory that supports this causal relationship is described in *The Trial of Steven Truscott* by LeBourdais:

> Dr. Allen discusses, among a number of subjects, the
> sadist, who is not, as popularly supposed, a person
> who enjoys being cruel all the time, but a person
> subject to periodic tensions which built up to a
> powerful urge to perform an act of extreme cruelty.
> The act relieves the tension and brings a feeling
> of peace until the tension grows again and leads
> to repetition.[8]

When I reviewed Talbot's personnel file at Industrial Plumbing, there were a number of memos that addressed poor work performance.[9] It is not a reach to assume these would have been stressful for Talbot:

> April 18, 1958: Sales report late.
> June 27, 1958: Sales report late.
> December 1, 1958: Demand to increase sales.
> February 10, 1959: Sales report late.
> October 27, 1961: Three holiday weeks cancelled
> by management.
> May 29, 1964: Critique — insufficient sales.
> November 24, 1964: Critique — sales slump.
> May 22, 1968: Demand for sales.
> May 23, 1968: Instructions from company president
> on work improvement.
> June 12, 1968: Memo from president — sales down.
> January 19, 1970: Demand to increase sales.
> Unknown month, 1970: Observation by manage-
> ment Talbot not coming to grips with new and
> difficult challenges.

In *Serial Killers*, author Peter Vronsky offered an explanation of why they are what they are:

> How and why do serial murderers kill again and
> again? Serial killing is an addiction, some experts
> say. Simply explained, once they begin killing, serial
> killers find themselves addicted to murder in an
> intense cycle that begins with homicidal sexual
> fantasies that in turn start a desperate search for
> victims, leading to their brutal killings, followed
> by a period of cooling off and a return to normal
> daily routine — with all its unbearable stresses,
> disappointments and hurts, which lead back to the
> re-emerging need to start fantasizing about killing
> again. Once a killing cycle is triggered, it is rarely
> broken. The worst aspect of this is that murder
> fantasies are often the only thing the budding serial
> killer has that gives him comfort and solace.[10]

When Det. Const. Mel Joa interviewed Talbot's sister, she said Talbot needed help because there was something wrong with him. According to a probation report dated September 24, 1979, Talbot himself told the probation officer he "feels that his conflicts with the law are the result of periods of depression in which he does not have an explanation or complete control." Talbot's sister told the probation officer she "strongly believed he was a voyeur and was entering cottages and stealing."[11]

An overview of Larry Talbot's criminal history reveals a troubled man who may indeed be capable of much more serious crimes than those for which he was convicted. As it was, he was found guilty of numerous crimes, including break and enter and armed robbery.

He had a propensity for violence and was armed with a large hunting knife and pellet gun when he broke into our cottage. He was known for prowling and voyeuristic activities at Sauble Beach. He was the prime suspect in the Pauline Dudley homicide. He was observed by surveillance cruising through a lover's lane at night. (On July 13, 1973 at 3:24 a.m., he was charged with speeding on Bartley Drive, in East York.) On several occasions, police found him in possession of a rape kit.

Could Talbot have been responsible for the murder of Lynne Harper? He was a troubled man, convicted and suspected of committing some very serious crimes. Steven Truscott on the other hand was a 14-year-old boy, unfairly targeted and ultimately arrested by Harold Graham.

I recall meeting Graham at the police funeral for my Uncle Jack (Whitty) at the time he was the Commissioner of the OPP. During his tenure, he introduced a number of progressive programs, including the recruitment of females. But he'll probably be most remembered for the role he played in the Lynne Harper homicide and the arrest of an innocent boy.

I was a proud member of the OPP for 30 years and, to a large extent, worked with dedicated officers. Wearing the blue requires individuals who possess the attributes needed to confront a situation and respond in a timely, effective manner.

Within the OPP, there is the elite Criminal Investigation Bureau (CIB). These members are on call 24-7 and away from home for extended periods of time. In 1959, Graham was a member of this elite bureau and assigned to an investigation which was to become iconic in the history of Canadian jurisprudence. He walked into the eye of a perfect storm in rural Ontario: A young girl was brutally murdered; the public were emotionally charged; he lacked the forensic tools available to the modern-day cop; and there was incredible pressure to solve the case. An article in the *Toronto Telegram* entitled "An Atrocity" highlighted the lynch mob mentality of the government at the time:

> The unprecedented size of the reward the Ontario
> government has offered and its urgent call for the
> capture of the killer dead or alive reflects the shock
> at the murder of Lynne Harper. ...That a child
> could lose her life in this way is a crime that is too
> appalling for a consideration of charity towards the
> criminal. As public outrage mounted, so did the
> unprecedented pressure on the police to solve this
> most horrible of crimes.[12]

Graham was probably assigned to the Harper homicide because he was a successful investigator. However, in the Truscott matter, he displayed a rush to judgment, fuelled by tunnel vision. In *Until You Are Dead*, Sher pointed this out when he referred to comments made by Graham, that were overheard by Dee Harris, the wife of Cpl. John Erskine, an identification officer assigned to the investigation:

> The officers would come back to our house ... I'd
> hear them talking about the pros and cons. She
> remembers one of the first visits ... at the very
> beginning of the investigation. Graham came in
> first, up the three stairs from the side-door landing
> toward her kitchen. "He's guilty!" the inspector
> declared as he turned to the men behind him. ...
> And when the officers left, her husband said: "I just

can't believe Graham would say he's guilty when the case has just started."[13]

It's not unreasonable to wonder if Graham's premature pronouncement at Erskine's influenced the investigators assisting him in the case.

Sher put this rush to judgment in perspective when he commented on "the remarkable swift operation. ... In less than twenty four hours, he had solved the headline-grabbing murder that had prompted the province to issue an unprecedented 'dead or alive' reward."[14]

What were some of the factors that adversely effected the investigation? Tunnel vision may have deprived the investigators of the ability to separate the wheat from the chaff. In other words, from almost the beginning, Graham set his sights on Truscott and never considered the possibility it could be someone else. Initially, he sent a bulletin to police jurisdictions requesting them to keep an eye out for a Chevrolet driven by a subject who might have scratches on his body. He also included the time of death as 9 p.m. But, Sher pointed out that once Graham jailed Steven, no further references to the 9 p.m. time of death was made.[15]

Graham's focus was on witnesses who supported the notion Truscott was responsible for the homicide, in particular Joceyln Gaudet and Arnold "Butch" George. Gaudet told police Truscott made a date with her to go to Lawson's Bush to look for newborn calves and George told investigators he was at Truscott's residence on Tuesday evening and Steven allegedly told him he went into Lawson's bush with Lynne looking for a cow and a calf. The statements obtained from Gaudet and George were accepted without any attempt to authenticate them. In *Until You Are Dead*, Sher commented:

She (Gaudet) gave at least three different statements to the police in twenty-four hours from Friday afternoon to Saturday, each more elaborate than the previous one. A week after she signed her official police statement, she added a fourth declaration.[16]

Equally puzzling is that Graham opted to take
Gaudet's story at face value. Before arresting Steven,
the police took no statements from any adults who
could corroborate or challenge her story.[17]

At the Appeal Court hearing the justices commented on
George's testimony:

> The new material has powerful impeachment
> potential. George's unconfirmed and unsupported
> evidence that the appellant asked him to lie for him
> and that the appellant admitted being at the side of
> Lawson's Bush with Lynne looking for a cow and
> calf could be rejected at a hypothetical new trial
> where the appellant could more fully and effectively
> explore George's credibility.[18]

The justices named the three statements George gave to police
when arriving at their decision:

- On June 11, he told Const. Hobbs, before Lynne's body was
found, he "saw Truscott and Harper on a cycle go toward
#8 Highway."
- On [unknown] date, in a binder labeled "Graham" found in
the Archives of Ontario, one summary reads: "Arnold George
13…Tues. — had supper, cut lawn. Went to swimming hole
about 7 p.m. — Wasn't there about fifteen minutes, when
Steve & Lynne biked north, Went for swim on east side of
bridge — I came home just before dusk — about 8:30 p.m.
Before that I went to Steve's house & chatted. He was babysitting. Didn't talk to him about Lynne"
- In a third statement, George told the police he lied in the first
two statements to protect Steven and didn't see him at the
bridge. The justices commented: "In its closing, the Crown
(initial trial) painted George in a very sympathetic light and
presented a plausible and almost laudable explanation for
George's initial lies to the police. George was depicted as
a very loyal friend who had first lied to help the appellant,

but who appreciated that after Lynne's body was found, he had to tell the police the truth, even if the truth hurt his good friend.[19]

In the matter of Gaudet's credibility, the appeal court heard from Sandra Stolzmann, who was a nursing student in Montreal and a roommate of Gaudet in the 1960s and testified Gaudet told her she lied at the trial. Stolzmann said Gaudet repeated: "They've got the wrong guy, they've got the wrong guy."[20]

Unlike Graham's star witnesses, Gaudet and George, Dougie Oates and Gord Logan told police they saw Steven and Lynne cross the bridge headed in the direction of Highway 8. Oates said he was hunting turtles at the time and they "passed within feet of me. ... There's no doubt in my mind I saw both of them." Logan told the investigators he was swimming about six hundred feet from the bridge. "It must have been 7:30 when I saw her and Steven. I am sure it was her."[21] Allan Oates, Dougie's brother, said he saw Steven standing alone on the bridge at 7:45 p.m. Another witness, nine-year-old Karen Daum, who was interviewed by the police after Truscott was arrested said she saw Steven and Lynne on the county road after hunting turtles with Dougie Oates. Daum said: "I knew Lynne Harper and Steve Truscott. Me and Doug [Oates] were coming up from the river and going to go home and I saw Lynne riding on the bar of the Truscott's boys bike [sic]. We were going home and they were coming towards the river."[22] Daum corroborated the statements of Oates and Logan and the police were probably concerned that this statement was obtained after Truscott was arrested. The justices commented on the crown's dilemma:

> By the time of Daum's interview, the police must
> have had some theory for proving that the appellant
> killed Lynne Harper. They would have known that
> Daum's statement regarding where they passed the
> appellant and Lynne was inconsistent with that
> theory. Indeed, Mr. Sayeau, formerly Constable
> Sayeau of the O.P.P., who was closely involved in
> the investigation of Lynne Harper's murder, testified

before our court that he understood and believed
the police view at the time to be that Daum was a
cute little girl but she had to be wrong.[23]

Ironically, George, in his third statement, corroborated Oates
and Logan's observations. He recalled a number of boys, who were
at the bridge and saw Steven and Lynne pass, heading in the direction of Highway 8.

> I went swimming after that. ... I asked the guys
> Gordie Logan, Richard Gellatly, Ken Geiger, Gary
> Geiger, Rob Harrington, Hessy Daum, Darrell,
> Gilks if they had seen Steve. *Some of them said they
> had seen him. Logan, or Gellatly and Ken Geiger I
> think said they had seen Steve with Lynne going down
> towards No. 8 Highway.* [Emphasis added]*[24]

It appears the police weren't interested in statements made by
the children at the bridge because their theory would have been in
jeopardy. Instead, they said Oates and Logan were lying to protect
Steven and, according to Sayeau, Daum "had to be wrong."[25]

John Lea, a criminologist at the Crime and Research department
at Middlesex University in London, England, said the following,
regarding pressure on the police to quickly identify a suspect:

> The danger is of course that at once evidence begins
> to point in the direction of a particular suspect,
> there may be other evidence that conflicts with this.
> There may be a tendency to ignore or downplay
> such evidence, not from bad intent but because the
> evidence clashes with a promising hypothesis that
> looks like it's leading to a result. A key question par-
> ticularly from the standpoint of prosecution (taking
> the case to court), is what checks and balances there
> are on any tendency by the investigators to rush
> conclusions and ignore evidence which conflicts
> with, or fails to corroborate their line of inquiry.[26]

There was a lack of "checks and balances" in the Harper investigation. The absence of a comprehensive examination of witnesses meant the investigation was incomplete. In other words, the puzzle was missing pieces.

There is no reason to suspect malice against Steven Truscott played any role in what unfolded. What possible malice could police have for a boy from small-town Ontario? But neither has there ever been an explanation for the shoddiness of the investigation — the evidentiary inconsistencies, both in terms of witnesses and physical evidence, and the failure to follow up on other leads or other potential suspects.

The fact remains that within a few short months of the crime, Graham's single-minded pursuit of Truscott persuaded a jury to falsely convict a 14-year-old for murder, ruining his life forever.

It was a different time then. Police procedures were not scrutinized to the degree they are now. The public was not familiar with criminal profiling or forensics, even the less sophisticated forms practiced at that time. If the police were convinced of guilt, then the public — and the jury — were willing to accept that they must be right. And everyone — police, public, and jury — wanted to believe that this horrific crime had been solved and that the perpetrator would be appropriately punished.

After the conviction, although there were undoubtedly lots of back-slaps and congratulations for a job well done in the police community, not all officers were happy about the outcome. Dee Harris, wife of John Erskine, the OPP identification officer "who, from almost the start of the investigation had his doubts about Steven's guilt," said her husband was crestfallen when he heard the verdict. "He was white. He couldn't believe it. He was quite emphatic that he was not guilty."[27] Most trials do not stay long in the public consciousness. There are, unfortunately, too many lurid new cases to grab headlines and the public's attention. But the Truscott/Harper case did not fade into the background. There were many people, high-profile people, who were outraged that a 14-year-old boy had been given the death penalty, an injustice they believed as heinous as the murder itself. Almost immediately, the protests began.

Just a few days after the sentence was handed down, iconic writer Pierre Berton composed "Requiem for a Fourteen-Year-Old," a poignant poem making the point that it was immoral to hang such a young boy. Berton's poem unleashed a storm "more violent than I have yet known" he wrote in a follow-up column.[28]

He was not alone. In January 1960, Prime Minister John Diefenbaker learned of the case, and now-declassified Cabinet minutes indicate "he had been shocked to see that a fourteen-year old … had been sentenced to hang."[29] As a result, the death sentence was rescinded on January 21, 1960, and commuted to life imprisonment.[30]

In 1963, when Truscott turned 18, he was transferred from the Ontario Training School for Boys in Guelph, Ont. to Collins Bay Penitentiary in Kingston. Meanwhile, there were leaves for appeals and judicial rulings on those applications that also kept the story in the headlines.

In 1966, Laurier LaPierre, co-host of CBC's This Hour Has Seven Days, a controversial newsmagazine program interviewed Doris Truscott and following the interview "… wiped tears from his eyes … less than three weeks later, LaPierre learned his contract wouldn't be renewed." Also in 1966, Isabel LeBourdais published The Trial of Steven Truscott, the most detailed and comprehensive account of the case the public had seen. It was highly critical of the OPP investigation, reignited huge national interest, and was a nightmare for the police. Although many officers involved in the original investigation, including Graham, were making significant advancements up the hierarchical ladder, certainly partly as a result of their "success" with the Truscott case, their work and their competency was now being challenged like never before.

It was the case that just wouldn't go away.

In 1969, after 10 years of incarceration, Truscott, then 24 years old, was granted parole and was released from prison. Because he lived under an assumed name, his personal life did not perpetuate the story, but he did get on with living. He eventually married, had three children, and worked as a millwright. Although he did not deny his true identity, he kept out of the public eye until 2000, when he appeared on CBC's *the fifth estate*.

The legal wheels also continued to turn and public interest remained high, spurred on by Julian Sher's book, *Until You Are Dead*, published in 2001, just weeks before the federal justice minister ordered a review of the case that came to be known as the Kaufman Inquiry. Justice Kaufman's 2004 ruling eventually led to the Ontario Court of Appeal hearing that, in August 2007, finally ruled, unequivocally, that there had been a "miscarriage of justice" in the Steven Truscott case. He was exonerated of the crime, and the cloud he had lived under for 48 years started to evaporate.

Reaction to the acquittal was restrained among police and justice officials, who had nothing specific to answer to because the Court of Appeal had made no effort to say who or what was responsible for the miscarriage. A few officials gave half-hearted responses to questions about the possibility of re-opening the case, but nothing was ever done. Was it because this cold case was just too cold ,or was it because the OPP was loathe to admit it had erred and did not want to tarnish some of its brightest stars?

It's impossible to know how many tragedies were born the night Lynne Harper died. Certainly the lives of two families were destroyed, but what of other potential consequences?

Steven Truscott didn't murder Lynne Harper, but someone did. Is it possible the OPP's failure to find the real killer meant he went on to kill again?

Did they become so entrenched and defensive about the Harper case that they overlooked the similarities between her case and others — notably the Pauline Ivy Dudley murder — that could have led to new suspects?

Did the bombardment of criticism they received on the Harper case create an institutional reluctance to pursue suspects such as Larry Talbot for other crimes?

Talbot finally piqued serious OPP interest after he called our home in July 2008 but as they soon found out, it was too little, too late. He died just two months later.

Larry Talbot went to his grave without being properly investigated. He was a viable suspect in the Dudley homicide and perhaps in many others, including Harper's, but is now well beyond the reach of authorities. The OPP's failure to act in a thorough, timely manner means the answers he might have provided will remain forever a mystery.

FOOTNOTES

CHAPTER ONE — TO SERVE PROTECT AND SURVIVE

1. -Provincial Court, Walkerton, December 17, 1971.
2. *Letter Commendation*-Comm. Eric Silk, December 13, 1971.
3. *Probation Report*, September 24, 1979. *Transcript*
4. *OPP Circular*- Composite Suspect- August 2, 1969.

CHAPTER TWO — ARRESTED DEVELOPMENT

1. Sher, Julian. *Until You Are Dead.* Toronto: Vintage Canada, 2002, 29.
2. Supreme Court of Ontario Trial, 1959, (http://www.cbc.ca/news/back round/Truscott/documents.html.)
3. Sher, 58.
4. Superior Court of Ontario Trial, 1959, Vol. 2, pp 142-144.
5. Sher, 59.
6. Interview Jocelyn Gaudet: Superior Court of Ontario Trial, 1959, Vol.2, pp 194-202.
7. Sher, 72.
8. Sher, 74-84

9. Superior Court of Ontario Trial, 1959, Vol. 4, p.607.
10. Sher, 75.
11. Superior Court of Ontario Trial, Vol. 2, pf. 276-277.
12. Sher, 85.
13. Magistrates Court Preliminary Hearing, 1959 (http: //www. cbc.ca/news/backround/Truscott/document. html) Vol.2, p. 316.
14. Trent, Bill with Steven Truscott, *Who Killed Lynne Harper?* Montreal-Toronto: Optimum Publishing Company Limited, 1979, 94.
15. Sher, 121.
16. Superior Court of Ontario Trial, 1959, Vol.2, pp 194-202.
17. Superior Court of Ontario Trial, 1959, Vol.2, p.284.
18. Trent, 87.
19. Superior Court of Ontario Trial, Vol.6 A, 1311-1312.
20. Superior Court of Ontario Trial, Vol. 6.A., 1335.
21. Superior Court of Ontario Trial, Vol. 6A, 1335.
22. Superior Court of Ontario, Vol. 6 A, 1496.
23. Superior Court of Ontario, Vol.6 A, 1505.
24. Le Bourdais, *The Trial of Steven Truscott*, Philadelphia and New York: JB Lippincott Company, 233.
25. Sher, 364.
26. Higley, Dawn, *OPP The History of the Ontario Provincial Police*, Toronto: The Queens Printer, 1984, 460.
27. Superior Court of Canada Hearing, 1966 (http://www.cbc. ca/news/back round/truscott/documents. html.)

CHAPTER THREE — PRIME SUSPECT

1. Halton Regional case 10886-73

CHAPTER FOUR — THE EPIHANY

1. The Halton Regional Police report-*Pauline Dudley Homicide*.
2. Vronsky, Peter, *Serial Killers*, Philadelphia: The Charles Press, 1995, 77.

3. http://www.fbi.gov/stats-services/publications/serialmurder. August 29/September 2, 2005.
4. Crime Report sent to General Headquarters, Toronto, January29, 1982.
5. Police don't have the slightest clue, *The Globe and Mail*, June 23, 1982, 4.
6. Toronto Police Circular-*Christine Prince Homicide*, No. 24, 1982.
7. Toronto Police synopsis- Prince, 16.
8. Delia Adriano Homicide, *Toronto Star*, November 9, 1981, A2.
9. Dropped his chainsaw, *Oakville Beaver*, http://www OakvilleBeaver.com
10. Map south western Ontario- customers Industrial Plumbing circled.
11. Les Church interview, February 3, 1983.
12. Audio recording — *Les Church*, February 4, 1983.
13. Crime Report sent to *OPP General Headquarters, Toronto*, March 15, 1983.
14. Feedback from personnel at OPP General Headquarters re: crime report, March 23, 1983.
15. Surveillance approved, *Nelson Kinkaid* March 31, 1983.
16. The Harper-Talbot hypothesis, *Nelson Kinkaid*.
17. Surveillance approval comments OPP General Headquarters personnel-
18. T*he Kaufman Inquiry*, OPP disclosure notes, February 2001, Vol. 3.
19. Surveillance cancelled, May 4, 1983.
20. Complaint *Larry Talbot*, May 9, 1983.
21. *Personnel Evaluation Report*, 20 August 81 to 08 Sept. 82.
22. *Personnel Evaluation Report*, 08 Sept. 82 to 22 Sept. 83.

CHAPTER FIVE — ON
THE ROAD AGAIN

1. *Personnel Evaluation Report*, 22 Sept.83 to18 Oct.84.

2. Six slaying's may be linked, *The Toronto Star*, January 8, 1984, A1.
3. ...I'm impressed with ... *Toronto Star*, A1.
4. ...I'll admit out of leads... *Toronto Star*, A1.
5. ...left her neatly folded coat... *Toronto Star*, A1.
6. Le Bourdais, Isabel, *The Trial of Steven Truscott*. Philadelphia and New York: JB Lippincott Company, 40.
7. *Federal Bureau of Investigation* Publication.
8. *Crime Report* January 14, 1994.

CHAPTER SIX — RETIRED AND REHIRED

1. *Crime Report*, 1997
2. Le Bourdais, Isabel, *The Trial of Steven Truscott*, Philadelphia and New York: JB Lippincott Company, 114.
3. *Superior Court of Ontario* Trial, 1959 (http:www cbc.ca/news/back ground/Truscott/documents.html) Vol.4, 84.
4. LeBourdais, 24.
5. LeBourdais, 83.
6. LeBourdais, 29.
7. Crime Report 223-78.
8. LeBourdais, Isabel, *The Trial of Steven Truscott*, Toronto and Montreal: McClelland and Stewart Limited, 76.
9. LeBourdais, 110
10. LeBourdais, Isabel, *The Trial of Steven Truscott*, Philadelphia and New York: JB Lippincott Company, 31.
11. Sher, Julian, *Until You Are Dead*. Toronto: Vintage Canada, 2002. pp10-11.
12. LeBourdais, 247.
13. Cameron, Stevie, *On the Farm*, Toronto: Vintage Canada, 2011, pp 256-257.
14. www.attorney general. jus.gov.on.ca, pdf/ 10, Campbell Summary.
15. Correspondence to *Det. Insp. Coughlin* March 28, 1998.

16. Correspondence from *Det. Insp. Coughlin*, November, 1998.

CHAPTER SEVEN — A PERSON OF DISINTEREST

1. Heather Bird, Insp. Jim Wilson working on case, *Toronto Sun*, July 6, 2000:1
2. *Journal notes*, October 14, 1998, 10.
3. *Journal notes*, November 30, 1998, 13.
4. ViCLAS: *OPP Review* (Winter 2007/08)12.
5. OPP to reopen fifty Unsolved Cases, *Toronto Star*, January 30, 1999.
6. Correspondence faxed to *Comm. Gwen Boniface*, March 2, 1999.
7. *Journal notes*, August 2006, 1999, 21.
8. *Journal notes*, October 7, 1999, 25.
9. *Journal notes*, October 7, 1999, 26.
10. *Journal notes*, October 7, 1999, 26.
11. *Journal notes*, October twenty six, 1999, 26.
12. Interview *Larry Talbot*, September 27, 2000.

CHAPTER EIGHT — THE KAUFMAN INQUIRY

1. Sher, Julian, *Until You Are Dead*. Toronto: Vintage Canada, 2001, 20.
2. *OPP reports* sent to Truscott's lawyers.
3. *Journal notes*, October 5, 2001.
4. *Journal notes*, February 3-4, 1983.
5. Briefs sent to *Justice Fred Kaufman*, February 28, 2003.
6. Correspondence sent to *Justice Fred Kaufman*, February 19, 2003.
7. *Journal Notes*, February 28, 2003. 82
8. *Journal Notes*, February 28, 2003. 83
9. Sher, 538-39.
10. Sher, 539.

11. Sher, 539.
12. Sher, 539.
13. Sher, 540.
14. Sher, 539.
15. Sher, 540.
16. Sher, 540.
17. *Kaufman Inquiry* P.652, Sec. 1982-1989.

CHAPTER NINE- LAST CHANCE FOR JUSTICE

1. Justice Delayed, *The Globe and Mail*, October 29, 2004.
2. They had me sentenced to death. *Globe and Mail.*
3. *Court of Appeal for Ontario: Truscott (Re), 2007.* Docket-C42726, Dr. *Michael Pollanen*, p.181, pp 1-71.
4. Ontario Court of Appeal: *Dr. Nicolas Diamand*, p.191-192, 75.
5. Ontario Court of Appeal: *Dr. Bernard Knight*, p.182-184, pp72-73.
6. Ontario Court of Appeal: *Dr. Werner Spitz*, p.166- 177, pp 66-77.
7. Ontario Court of Appeal: *Entomology evidence*, p. 309-310, 120.
8. Ontario Court of Appeal: *Dr. Elgin Brown*, p. 309-310, 120.
9. Ontario Court of Appeal: *Dr Neil Haskell*, p.313, pp1212-1222.
10. Sher, Julian, *Until You Are Dead*, Toronto: Vintage Canada, 2002, p.555
11. Sher ,555.
12. Sher, 555.
13. Le Bourdais, Isabel, *The Trial of Steven Truscott*, Philadelphia and New York: JB Lippincott Company, 227.
14. Sher, 557.
15. Sher, 557.

16. *Ontario Court of Appeal Hearing*, 2007-2008. (http://www. cbc.ca/news/back round/Truscott/documents, html) p. 678, 261.
17. *Ontario Court of Appeal, p.1215-1216, pp 816-817.*
18. *Ontario Court of Appeal, p.1300, pp 681-682.*
19. *Ontario Court of Appeal, p.1292, pp 676-677.*
20. *Ontario Court of Appeal, p. 288, 188.*
21. *Ontario Court of Appeal, p.288, 111.*
22. *Ontario Court of Appeal, p.776, 299.*
23. *Ontario Court of Appeal, p.776, 299.*
24. *Ontario Court of Appeal, p.778, 300.*
25. Ontario Court of Appeal, p.779, 300.
26. *Superior Court of Ontario Trial*, 1959. (http://www.cbvc.ca/ news/bacd round/Truscott/documents. html) Vol.2, p.355, 55; p.382, 83; p.390, 91; p.364, 65.
27. *Ontario Court of Appeal, p.780, 300.*
28. *Ontario Court of Appeal, p.781, 301.*
29. *Ontario Court of Appeal, p.782, 301.*
30. *Ontario Court of Appeal, p.787, 302-303.*
31. The Long Journey for Vindication… *The London Free Press*, August 29, 2007.
32. OPP could reopen search … *The National Post*, August 27, 2007.
33. I know he apologized on behalf … *The London Free Press*, August 29, 2007.

CHAPTER TEN — LAST CALL

1. Tracey Tyler Other leads on possible suspects, *The Toronto Star*, August 29, 2007.
2. *The Kaufman Inquiry*, Vol. 2, 342-451.
3. ViCLAS, *The OPP Review*, Winter 2007/08. 12
4. OPP Circular, *Lea Sousa homicide* No. 151-90, September 1, 1990.

CHAPTER ELEVEN — A VIABLE SUSPECT BEYOND REACH

1. The Kaufman Inquiry, *A Summary of "Other Suspects,"* P.652, Section 1982-1989.
2. The Kaufman Inquiry, *A Comparative Analysis, the Harper and Dudley crime scenes.*
3. Holmes, Ronald and Holmes, Stephen T. *Profiling Violent Crimes.* California: Sage Publications Inc., 2002, 44.
4. LeBourdais, Isabel *The Trial of Steven Truscott*, Philadelphia and New York: JB Lippincott Company, 1966, 288.
5. Sher, Julian. *Until You Are Dead.* Toronto: Vintage Canada, 2002, 11.
6. Holmes and Holmes, 76.
7. Holmes and Holmes, *The Holmes Typology (Part 1)* Adapted and modified from R. Holmes (1996) Profiling Violent Crimes.
8. LeBourdais, 232.
9. *Personnel file of Larry Talbot* from Industrial Plumbing.
10. Vronsky, Peter. *Serial Killers*, New York: Berkley Books, 2003, pp11-12.
11. *Probation Report* of Larry Talbot, September 24, 1979.
12. The Toronto Telegram in Sher, 2001, 70.
13. Sher, 2001, 94.
14. Sher, 2001, 93.
15. Sher, 2002, 59.
16. Sher, 2001, 75.
17. Sher, 2001, 76.
18. *Court of Appeal for Ontario: Truscott (Re), 2007.* Docket-C42726, P.562.
19. *Ontario Court of Appeal.* P.532-535-545.
20. Sher. 2002, 555.
21. Sher. 2001, 33.
22. *Ontario Court of Appeal. P.687.*
23. *Ontario Court of Appeal. P.715.*
24. *Ontario Court of Appeal. P.558.*

25. *Ontario Court of Appeal. P.467.*
26. *Lea, John*, (http://www.bunker8.pwp.blueyonger.co.uk/ cjs/26903.htm.)
27. Sher, 2002, 268.
28. Sher, 2002, 312-13.
29. Sher, 2002, 309.
30. Sher, 2002, 318.

REFERENCES

Appelby T. (2011) A New Kind of Monster, Vintage-Canada, 193.

attorney general. Jus. gov. on .ca Campbell Summary-pdf.

Cameron, S. (2011). On the Farm, Toronto, Vintage Canada. 106-107.

Crime Report (1978) Larry Talbot arrested "Possession of Burglary Tools" Investigating officer Const. John Olmstead, Wiarton OPP.

Crime Report (1983) Requesting an investigation of Larry Talbot for a number of unsolved homicides (excluding Lynne Harper.)

Crime Report (1994) sent to Detective Inspector Barry Thompson requesting an investigation of Larry Talbot for the Cindy Halliday homicide.

Crime Report (1997) Requesting an investigation of Larry Talbot for the murder of Lynne Harper and a number of other women.

Department of Justice Canada, (2002) Executive Summary- Report for the Minister of Justice prepared by the Honorable Fred Kaufman, 10.

FBI National Centre of the Analysis of Violent Crime Handbook.

Globe and Mail (2002) Appeal Court to hear evidence at future date.

Halton Regional Police Circular- Pauline Ivy Dudley Homicide.

Halton Regional Report(s) sent to me reference Larry Talbot "Prime Suspect" in the Dudley homicide.

Halton Regional Police circular- Delia Adriano homicide- Case #67034-82

Higley, D. (1984) OPP -The History of the Ontario Provincial Police.   Toronto: The Queens Printer, 460.

Holmes R. and Holmes S. (2002) Profiling Violent Crimes. Thousand Oaks, California: Sage Publications Inc. 44.

Journal notes accumulated during my conversations with members of the Ontario Provincial Police.

The Kaufman Inquiry (2001) Testimony from the Inquiry.

Le Bourdais, I. (1966) The Trial of Steven Truscott. Philadelphia and New York: JB Lippincott Company, 228.

Kaufman Journal (2001) Notes relevant to my testimony and conversation with Mark Sandler, assisting Kaufman at the Inquiry.

Letter of Commendation (1971) from Comm. Eric Silk for the arrest of Talbot following the break in at our cottage.

London Free Press (2007) Truscott found not responsible for the Harper homicide.

Magistrates Court (1959) Preliminary Hearing Steven Truscott before Justice Holmes.

Map of Ontario (1983) shown to Les Church and locations visited, while employed by Industrial Plumbing.

Mellor L. (2012) Cold North Killers Toronto, Dundurn Press, 236.

National Post (2007) Truscott found not responsible for Harper's murder and Comm. Fantino to meet with personnel from the Attorney General's office, to ascertain if a new investigation would be conducted regarding the Lynne Harper homicide.

Ontario Court of Appeal (1960) Following Truscott's trial and guilty verdict. Appeal dismissed.

Ontario Court of Appeal (2007) The appeal was allowed and the conviction for murder was set aside.

OPP Disclosure Brief (2001) Obtained by James Lockyer in preparation for the Kaufman Inquiry. Included: the 1997 Crime Report; the Behavioral Sciences Unit analysis of Larry Talbot, and the Interview Report obtained from Talbot by Detective Sgt. Pauline Schwantz.

OPP Circular (1969) Composite drawing of perpetrator who sexually assaulted a hitch hiker in the Owen Sound area.

OPP Circular (1990) Leah Sousa homicide- #151-90.

Personnel Evaluation Report (20 Aug.81-08 Sept.82)

Personnel Evaluation Report (1982-83)

Personnel Evaluation Report (1983-84)

Prince, Christine homicide (1982) circular

TIME LINE — THE 1997 REPORT

March 28, 1998 I gave Det. Insp. Mike Coughlin of the Criminal Investigation Branch a copy of the report. He sent it to "Project Angel" in London. A copy was also forwarded to Det. Insp. Jim Wilson investigating "persons of interest" who came to the attention of the authorities, after Steven Truscott volunteered to undergo a DNA examination. (It's unknown when Wilson received the report.)

November 30, 1998 I contacted Wilson regarding the status of the report. He was very busy with a number of investigations and said he would read the report in two months.

December 4, 1998 I met with Det. Supt. Larry Edgar, Wilson's supervisor. I expressed my concern regarding Wilson's response. He was going to speak to him and would call in "a couple of weeks." I gave him two copies of the report and he was going to give one to his supervisor Chief Supt. Wayne Frechette and the other to the Behavioural Science Unit.

January 15, 1999 I never received a call from Edgar, and contacted him. He spoke to Wilson and requested that I call him in the future, instead of Wilson.

February 5, 1999 I called Edgar for an update on the status of the report. He told me Wilson was working on a missing person investigation in New Liskeard. He suggested I call the following Monday, when the officers call and update him on their investigations.

February 9, 1999 I contacted Edgar and he hadn't talked to Wilson, but he would page him, and call me back. I never received a call.

February 16, 1999 Wilson called my residence when I wasn't home. My wife told him I was in Toronto and would be home the following day. He told her he was going away on business and would contact me at a later date.

February 18, 1999 I called Wilson and left a message on his voice mail to contact me. He never returned my call.

March 2, 1999 My lawyer faxed a letter to Comm. Gwen Boniface and Dep.Comm. Moe Pilon. He expressed a concern regarding the lack of progress in the investigation.

March 2, 1999 I received a voice mail from Frechette. He was forwarding the report to the Behavioural Science Unit for analysis "in terms of linkages and similarities" and when he received the results, he'd decide what to do with it.

July 8, 1999 I received a voice mail from Staff Sgt. Mary McLaughlin. She was reviewing the file and wanted to meet with me.

July 19, 1999 McLaughlin called and told me Halton Regional, Durham Regional and "Project Angel" were interested in Talbot. She was advised by Sgt. Steve Smethurst, an analyst in the Behavioural Science Unit, Talbot may be linked to three homicides, with the potential for others.

September 1, 1999 I had a meeting with McLaughlin at my residence. It began at 11:15 a.m. and concluded at 2:45 p.m. I reviewed the report, including the circumstantial evidence implicating Talbot in the Lynne Harper homicide. (She had no opinion regarding the Harper homicide and needed to complete some research including the LeBourdais book and CIB files.)

September 22, 1999 McLaughlin called and had contacted the Halton Regional Police who were reluctant to give her any information on the Dudley homicide. She was going to contact the Centre of Forensic Sciences, to determine if the hair seized from Talbot's vehicle was sent to them for examination.

October 7, 1999 I received a call from McLaughlin and she was reviewing the files we discussed at our September 1 meeting. She was also reviewing the homicide of a woman from Smith Falls, who was stabbed to death in the 1970's, because Talbot was known to carry knives. She recovered a report in the archives I sent Det. Insp. Barry Thompson regarding the Cindy Halliday homicide and didn't know if anyone was assigned to the case following his death.

She advised me she wouldn't be investigating the Lynne Harper case and hadn't read any of the reports because Wilson was investigating the Truscott matter. She was following up on the other cases but only in her spare time as she had other assignments and was also required for court in Owen Sound and Lindsay.

(I told McLaughlin I wasn't happy because the OPP were dragging their feet. I contacted my lawyer, who spoke with a command staff member at General Headquarters.)

October 26, 1999 McLaughlin called me and sounded upset. She was disappointed I made the call and said she had contacted me a number of times regarding the investigation. She also said she told me a couple of times she wasn't investigating the Harper matter. She also told me she had to write a report regarding the conversations she had with me. She was going to request removal from the investigation. I never heard from her following this conversation.

September 27, 2000 Thirty months after the OPP received my report Det. Sgt. Pauline Schwantz interviewed Talbot in his kitchen, with his wife present. The interview commenced at 12:25 p.m. and concluded at 13:04 p.m. Talbot was asked 13 questions regarding the Lynne Harper homicide. He was asked if he would submit to a polygraph examination. He replied in the affirmative. It wasn't done.

July 1, 2008 Larry Talbot called my residence and spoke to my wife. Det. Insp. Chris Gilpin was assigned to investigate Talbot. She was in the process of reviewing the reports and documents I gave to the OPP and was going to interview Talbot, along with officers from Halton Regional and Toronto police on September 14. He died on September 8.

ACKNOWLEDGEMENTS

I'm very grateful to my family especially my lifelong partner Pat, who was my sounding board during the writing process, despite the fact that this required her to relive the victimization by Larry Talbot. She is stronger than you can imagine.

Thanks also to my son Jeff and his wife Danielle, my brother Doug and his wife Val, and my brother Phil for their advice and support.

I was very fortunate to have Susan Greer as an editor. Suffice to say, she transformed the "needy" manuscript.

In view of the book's controversial nature, I consulted with counsel Brian Rogers and appreciate his review of the work and the advice we received.

When the initial draft was completed, crime writer James Dubro reviewed it and identified *many* changes required before it could be ready for publication.

I also appreciate the advice and encouragement I received from Mark Murphy, RCMP (Ret.), who shared his journey when he wrote "Police Undercover."

I'm also grateful to a number of friends who read the manuscript and offered suggestions: Maddi Damico, Bill Darrin, Mark Evans, Jim Barlow, Roch Berniquez, George Plant, Ron and Margie Rogers and Mike Epstein.

Authors Isabel LeBourdais (*The Trial of Steven Truscott*), Bill Trent (*The Steven Truscott Story*), Julian Sher (*Until You Are Dead*) and Nate Hendley (*Steven Truscott, Decades of Injustice*) helped me better understand the forces at work that contributed to the miscarriage of justice.

From the beginning, my relationship with Friesen Press was excellent. They were friendly, supportive and eager to assist when I had questions or concerns.

PHOTO CREDITS

AUTHOR'S PERSONAL ARCHIVE

CHAPTER 1: To Serve Protect and Survive
"Welcome to Sauble Beach" signage
Pat Elliott Ruhl

CHAPTER 2: Arrested Development
County Road Bridge leading to Highway 8
Lawson's Bush
Gravesite of Lynne Harper

CHAPTER 3: Prime Suspect
Barry Ruhl undercover
Barry Ruhl in uniform, 1970

CHAPTER 4: The Epiphany
Map of locations visited by Les Church* for Industrial Plumbing*

OTHER SOURCES

Location in Lawson's Bush where Lynne
Harper was murdered- George Plant

Photograph of Lynne Harper — Ontario Public Archives

Photograph of Barry Ruhl and Steven Truscott- Bent Romnes

1957 Chevrolet — Old Car Manual Project

1959 Chevrolet — Supreme Court of Ontario-The
Queen vs. Steven Murray Truscott- Exhibit 15

Items used by Larry Talbot for the break in at our cottage —
District Six Identification Unit, Ontario Provincial Police.

Door panel smashed during entry by Larry Talbot — District
Six Identification Unit, Ontario Provincial Police.

Identification photo of Larry Talbot-District Six
Identification Unit, Ontario Provincial Police.

Surveillance photo of Larry Talbot-District Six
Identification Unit, Ontario Provincial Police.

Photograph of Pat and Barry Ruhl-Platinum
Studio, Santa Clara California

Photograph of Barry Ruhl — Platinum
Studio, Santa Clara California

OTHER DOCUMENTS

Pauline Ivy Dudley circular. Oakville Police
Department (Halton Regional Police Service.)

Interview of Larry Talbot Staff Sgt. Pauline
Schwantz- Ontario Provincial Police.

Letter of Commendation — Comm. Eric. H. Silk

Toronto Star article-"Other leads on possible suspects ignored."

CPSIA information can be obtained at www.ICGtesting.com
Printed in the USA
LVOW07s1526170215

427301LV00002B/114/P